All the Good Ones Are Not Taken

ALL the GOOD ONES Are *Not* TAKEN

A Guide for Women Over 50 Looking For Fabulous Love

Linda Yalen

NEW YORK

LONDON • NASHVILLE • MELBOURNE • VANCOUVER

ALL the GOOD ONES Are Not TAKEN

A Guide for Women Over 50 Looking For Fabulous Love

Published in New York, New York, by Morgan James Publishing in partnership with Difference Press. Morgan James is a trademark of Morgan James, LLC. www.MorganJamesPublishing.com

The Morgan James Speakers Group can bring authors to your live event. For more information or to book an event visit The Morgan James Speakers Group at www.TheMorganJamesSpeakersGroup.com.

ISBN 9781683508359 paperback
ISBN 9781683508366 eBook
Library of Congress Control Number: 2017917245

Cover & Interior Design by:
Christopher Kirk
www.GFSstudio.com

NOTE: The content of this book is for general instruction only. Each person's physical, emotional and spiritual condition is unique. The instruction in this book is not intended to replace or interrupt the reader's relationship with a physician or other professional, and your doctor should be consulted for matters pertaining to your specific health and diet.

In an effort to support local communities, raise awareness and funds, Morgan James Publishing donates a percentage of all book sales for the life of each book to Habitat for Humanity Peninsula and Greater Williamsburg.

Get involved today! Visit
www.MorganJamesBuilds.com

I dedicate this book to all the beautiful women in the world who give of themselves to others. Your tireless dedication to making the world a better place without asking for anything in return is the reason I choose to work with you. You are deserving of just as much as you give. It is time to take care of you without hesitation!

FOREWORD

Linda puts together all the experiences she's had and studies she has undertaken to come up with a comprehensive plan to—get out there, in every way! Whether it's for love, or love of life, discovering and living your authentic self is essential to success. It's a cautionary tale as well, and may prevent her readers from making some of the same mistakes. A lifetime of learning distilled, for her lucky readers.

Bear McKay
Director of The McKay Method School of Energy Healing

ADVANCE PRAISE

"I was very impressed with the book. There is so much information that anyone can put themselves in any situation described. I personally enjoyed every aspect of the book. I believe every women should read it and any man if they wanted a different and truthful perspective. It is so well written and kept me interest to the very end, I wanted more." *~Maryanne R.*

"Fabulous read! I just loved the book, the insight into discovering oneself is great. Not only is this book great for singles but for women in general for developing personal self-awareness. Thank you Linda for your wisdom and knowledge!!" *~Nancy T.*

"Wow! Linda writes from the heart and gets you to move forward with an open heart and self-love—giving women the tools to create a healthy, loving relationship. A must read for all women looking to enhance their love lives." *~Gigi R.*

"This is more than just a book on dating! Linda shares her knowledge, experiences and training on how your mind and beliefs impact your body and behavior. You learn that cultivating an awareness of how you operate in the world can positively transform your life experiences. As you begin to allow yourself to be more comfortable with taking reasonable risks and trying new things, you can become liberated from your fears and preconceived notions of the experience of meeting new people. She challenges you to redefine what you have convinced yourself are roadblocks and you discover that often you are the one standing in the way of opening up to generating meaningful companionship. She also provides great suggestions on where to meet a potential mate in common places and thorough advice on navigating the world of online dating."   *~Denise B.*

"As a relationship coach, I was impressed with the down to earth, practical, and easy to understand way the author talks about our body's energy centers and the way each center plays into our success in a relationship. Yalen also offers excellent practical guidance for navigating the online dating world. If you are over 50 and looking for some solid advice in finding a successful relationship, start with Linda's book, and prepare for the positive changes heading your way!"   *~Cindi H.*

"I absolutely became addicted to this book at the get go! Learning about the seven energy levels (Chakras) was my favorite part of the book. Taking the self-assessment quizzes was so cool. The suggestions in activities to help balance the "Chakra" was helpful. There are some that I am already doing and others that I started to incorporate into my lifestyle i.e. gardening, fasting, acupuncture. This book lets you reflect about yourself and helps to get you to the next level of becoming a better and healthier you."   *~Ella J.*

"Linda shares her experiences and her knowledge in this book. It keep you engaged and most of all makes you feel valuable and worth investing in yourself and what you deserve. It opens up the mind to options of potential changes you can make to reinvent yourself in a positive thinking way."   *~Allison S.*

TABLE OF CONTENTS

Introduction 1

Chapter 1—Once Upon a Time 3

Chapter 2—Developing a Diamond Mindset 9

    Relationship Assessment 9

    Relationship ABCs 10

    The W.I.S.E™ Method. 11

    Beliefs and Behaviors 12

Chapter 3—Assess Your Beliefs 15

    The Seven Energy Centers 15

    First Chakra—The Root (Family & Security). 16

    Second Chakra—The Sacral (Creativity & Sexuality). 23

    Third Chakra—The Solar Plexus (Wisdom & Power). 28

    Fourth Chakra—The Heart (Love & Healing). 32

    Fifth Chakra—The Throat (Communication) 37

    Sixth Chakra—The Third Eye (Intuition & Awareness) 39

    Seventh Chakra—The Crown (Spirituality). 42

    The Grounding Technique. 46

Chapter 4—Behavior Assessment 49

    The Five Personality Types. 51

    Creative/Schizoid (The Creator) 51

    Empathetic/Oral (The Communicator) 55

Nurturer/Masochist (The Endurer) 60

Leader/Psychopath (The Controller) 64

Achiever/Rigid 67

Chapter 5—Balance 73

Chapter 6—Change 77

Chapter 7—Dating over 50 82

Online Dating 100

Chapter 8—Learning to Love Again 111

Chapter 9—A Healthier You! 116

Essential Oils and Hormone Health 117

Adrenal Fatigue 117

Depression 119

Hypothyroidism 120

Menopause 122

Premenstrual Syndrome (PMS) 123

Weight Gain/Obesity 124

Effective Oils 125

DIY Recipes 127

Chapter 10—The Best Possible You! 130

Successful Love Begins at Home 131

Conclusion 135

FAQ's About Coaching 137

References 139

Acknowledgments 141

About the Author 142

INTRODUCTION

I wish I knew then what I know now. We've all heard that saying, and for many, it has a different meaning. But in reality, we were meant to experience life at every stage, to learn from our experiences, as it is the only way to grow. Those experiences were made to teach us something of value, so we can avoid repeating the same mistakes. Learning from your past mistakes gives you insight into your personality, your strengths, your weaknesses, and what makes you happy. It is your journey of resilience, strength, and courage. There are two requirements needed to grow, change, and be at peace with who you are: acknowledgment and courage. Both strengthen your resilience in life and love.

I have experienced many of the same relationship ups and downs as you. If you have spent your life searching for compatible love, it is time to embrace your authentic self and finally identify what you might have been struggling with for most, if not all of your life, and find a mate who will love you for who you are today.

This book is written to help women over 50 solve their relationship challenges by identifying and embracing that which makes them unique and fabulous, not only to the outside world, but most importantly to themselves. I have an objective, and that is to bring out the best in you. I want you to realize that life can be amazing at our age! It can be simple, complex, or anything in between. Whatever it is for you, I will help you get there by acknowledging and validating your best qualities and helping you see that your authentic self has something to offer, something that a man is searching for. We are all unique, and once you begin to embrace and celebrate your authenticity, you will see the possibilities of finding and keeping a good man, one that you would never have imagined you would find at this time in your life.

Let's take this journey together. Let's push any negativity out of the way and let the sun shine in. Let's:

Turn bitter into better!

Turn crappy into happy!

Turn sassy into classy! Turn dabbler into doer!

Turn "woe is me" into "wow is me"!

There is no better time to make changes than right now. I promise there is no downside to any of this! There is no reason for you to feel lost, sad, or even indifferent. There are men searching for the same things you are. Where are they? They might be right around the corner, behind you in a grocery checkout line, at Home Depot, or waiting in the prepared food section at Whole Foods. So take a deep breath, clear your thoughts, and begin to clear that hazy filter you've been looking through. There are gifts presented to you every day, and it is my wish for you to be able to spot those gifts with clarity. It is all in the mindset you choose. It's like the difference between coal and a diamond. Both are made of the same material, but depending on the circumstances, the coal remains coal or becomes a diamond. Our mindset is the same: The choice of how you view the world can be either that of a lump of coal or a brilliant diamond. It's time to claim your fabulous self and give yourself the space to continue to grow and live the life you want and deserve.

Chapter 1
ONCE UPON A TIME

I was born in 1956 and grew up as a baby boomer in a typical middle-class family. My parents raised four children, and life was good. As a young teen, I dated in high school and had a few boyfriends during those four years. One relationship was traumatic; the other was not. In both cases and for differing reasons, things began to unravel at about the six-month mark. Although both of these relationships took place when I was 16, it was the beginning of a lifelong programmed pattern.

The first real boyfriend I ever had was a year older, and one of the most popular sports figures in school. He was charming and charismatic, with a strong, stocky build. I used to pass him in the hall every morning while he was standing around with his buddies. One morning, I had the nerve to say "Hi," and once he knew I had an interest in him, he didn't hesitate to respond. And so, our high school dating journey began.

It wasn't long before the verbal abuse started, yet I continued to be drawn to his charismatic charm. After only three months, it became a daily ritual for him to belittle me in public as well as verbally abuse me on the phone. I continued to date him. What was I drawn to? I would often think, "If Dad knew, he'd protect me from him," yet I never spoke to my father about it. Why did I feel the need to continue with this relationship? It was as my thoughts and feelings were not valued, my voice was silent and I would rather have negative attention than no attention—I was incomplete without a guy in my life. It was also the beginning of a "victim" mentality, one which I would not understand until 35 years later.

I stayed in the relationship for another six months (which seemed like a lifetime back then), and the emotional abuse started turning a bit violent. Thankfully, it only took one last instance before I had the guts to say, "Enough is enough." I was riding in the passenger seat of his car and we were chatting. The next thing I knew I felt a stinging across my face as he backhanded me because I spoke up. After he dropped me off at home I decided that I had to get away from him. I remember how empowered I felt meeting him in the hallway at school the next day, handing him a bag with everything he ever gave me, and saying, "I'm done." And I did it in front of everyone, just like he had done to me for the past six months. It was my first lesson in self-love, and it felt great! He begged me to come back to him, but I never hesitated to say no. I couldn't wait until he graduated so I didn't have to see him ever again.

My second boyfriend came on the heels of the first one, and I couldn't have found someone who was more of a polar opposite. Frank was gentle and kind, respectful and loving. We had many high school couple friends we'd hang out with. This group was made up of rebellious hippie types, and so I went from hanging in the lobby to hanging in the parking lot and cutting school. Although we were quite compatible and had lots of fun, my parents did not like Frank and forbade me to date him, as I was beginning to slack off on my schoolwork, right around college application time. After about six months, our relationship ended when Frank went off to college and I entered my senior year of high school.

My third boyfriend had no ambition. I don't recall ever having a decent conversation with him, as he was a bit older than me and didn't do much for work. It was the mid 70's and hanging around smoking pot and doing nothing wasn't a big deal. I never liked smoking pot, so I was ridiculed by my boyfriend and his friends for being a "prude". It was the holiday season, and we decided to buy each other hiking boots. I was so sick of him by that time that I sold his boots to a friend. I broke up with him after he gave me the hiking boots; at least I got something of value!

When it came time to graduate, I attended a court reporting certification program instead of attending college and headed to Boston two years later to live with my older sister. I landed a job in a law firm and decided to stay. I loved living in Boston in my early 20s!

I spent the next few years having fun, working, and building my career. It was a nice balance. Then one beautiful August evening as I was walking home from a night out with my friends, my life turned on a dime. I was accosted by a stranger who sexually assaulted me. I was 23 years old.

I was left with a wound that both echoed my first abusive boyfriend and that would also guide my relationship choices going forward. I lost trust in men and came to believe that sex was dirty and violent, as I had never experienced an emotional connection with any man to validate the beauty and sacred intimacy between two people who truly loved each other. I didn't know that at the time, however. I just knew I needed to remove myself from the connection I had made to the city and the event. Shortly after that, I relocated to Hartford and landed a job.

I hadn't given much thought to relationships; sex was the farthest thing from my mind. But after a short period, I did meet someone, and I was attracted to him because of his protective strength. I was still fragile after the trauma, and I thought I needed a man to protect me and keep me safe. We were married three years after we met. I was a good wife, had two beautiful daughters, and felt privileged to stay home with my children. I took care of the household and finances. But there was always something missing, and that was the emotional connection to my husband. It was like I was operating on autopilot, protecting myself from feeling anything and the risks that might come with having a voice. I lacked any communication skills, especially when it came to my own emotional needs. It couldn't have been easy for him either, I had so much fear in me about rejection. It's true, what you believe is what you see, and my filter was glazed over with continuing to be invisible.

For the next 15 years I was still struggling with my self-worth. I often wondered what it was like to be in a mutually loving relationship where I could flourish. I felt lost and invisible. Why was I always feeling like a victim? One day I was watching TV, as I usually did every afternoon while the kids were in school, and I came upon an interesting PBS special hosted by Carolyn Myss, a well-known medical intuitive. I had never heard of energy medicine and the chakras, and as I watched, I was completely engaged by the content. Carolyn had a way of explaining energy medicine that made sense to a novice. It was at that moment that I realized it was the key to understanding and healing the wound I had been carrying around for 15 years. I also knew it was not going to be easy, but I was at a point where I had nothing to lose. I was done feeling sad and disconnected.

So I began to take an inventory of my life. I knew I had low self-esteem, was a people pleaser, never spoke up for myself, and had a history of making relationship choices based on those areas. One thing I noticed was that every relationship I'd been in had been different from the last, and I realized that I was doing something all along, I was not making the same mistake twice. I was simply acting from my beliefs and needs at the time. So as my programmed beliefs changed due to life experiences, so did my dating choices.

I bought every book and audio tape Carolyn Myss had written or produced, and I began my healing journey. I had to find the courage to make drastic changes in my life, one of which included my marriage. So after 17 years of marriage, I filed for divorce. I had no job, and I was raising my two daughters who were both in elementary school, but I knew I had to advocate for my own happiness.

As soon as I was separated from my husband (I was 46 years old), I jumped back into the dating scene again. It was 2003, and online dating was relatively new. There was only one site that I was aware of, and that was Match.com. Since I didn't have any decent dating experiences, I was unsure of what to write about myself and what picture to post. The photo I chose was of me sitting by the fireplace with a winter sweater, a photo that would attract a nice man. I was technically still married, so I disclosed that I was separated (not divorced) in my profile, which did not play in my favor. I got responses that were varied: one guy wanted to rub oil all over my body, while another I had initiated contact with told me that there was no way he wanted to be a "rebound" guy. It was confusing, to say the least! I felt discouraged and lost. I was slowly learning to gain a sense of self-worth, but the world couldn't see it. Why did I place any value on the limited experience I was having with online dating?

After accepting dates from anyone who seemed nice, I began to see the same pattern in myself that I carried with me my whole life, that of being a people pleaser. I didn't know how to say no to anyone. I also didn't know how to change it, and it became more and more of a hindrance as I began to allow myself the space to acknowledge what was not working for me anymore, and never had. I didn't know how to get out of my own way! So I did what I hadn't done in quite a while—I began to pray.

Prayer was always something I did when I was lost or in trouble. I was not used to praying with gratitude every day, which is something I now do regularly. This time, my prayer wasn't asking for a good man, as I had before, it was asking for guidance. I took a walk in the woods, stopped at a split-rail fence, looked around to make sure no one was around, and I looked up to the sky with tears in my eyes and said, "God, please show me the way, please guide me to do the right thing."

At that moment I heard a voice say, "Put the check in the mail."

Wait, that's the answer I got? What in the world did it mean? So I repeated it to myself, having no clue what it was about. I'm supposed to put a check in the mail ... huh? Then, suddenly, it came to me as clear as day: I was ready to put the check to my divorce attorney in the mail!

So I went back home, wrote the check, and dropped it in the mailbox at the post office that evening. What I was doing was following the guidance I received without question. That night, I removed my profile picture from Match.com with the intention of reevaluating my dating choices. The very next day, I received a message on Match.com from a man who had read my picture-free profile. We spoke, we met, and we fell in love. I am still with him today, and we just celebrated our 14th year of being together. Apparently listening to my intuition was paying off!

During the time my daughters were growing up, I spent time getting certifications in what was of interest to me. The first one was a two-year certification in energy medicine from the Institute of Healing Arts & Sciences in 2009. The second was a certification as a health/life coach in 2015 from the Institute of Integrative Nutrition, and the third and most recent one, an Essential Oil Coach from The Essential Oil Institute, taught by Dr. Josh Axe. These certifications paved the way for me to help women with both health and relationship challenges. I loved seeing my clients not only thrive, but also become the empowered women they always deserved to be. There were only two requirements, that they have the willingness to change and have the courage to implement those changes. The rest would fall into place!

Chapter 2
DEVELOPING A DIAMOND MINDSET

"A diamond is a lump of coal that did well under pressure"

– Henry Kissinger

Relationship Assessment

My story in the last chapter reveals the blueprint I had been using during my young adulthood to make relationship choices. I had been basing those choices on my lack of self-esteem and on being a "people pleaser," always putting myself last. I had invested in bad choices for relationship partners my whole life. But finally, through the knowledge of energy medicine, I found the courage to step out of my comfort zone and make choices based on what was best for me. I realized that my behavior patterns had consistently undermined my happiness for most of my adult life—and that it was never too late to learn from those mistakes.

To learn from your relationship experiences, you have to acknowledge the truth about each one of them. It's important to be able to take inventory of both your beliefs in relationships and your past behavior and choices. One of the first things to do for yourself is to give yourself a break for your past, acknowledging any regrets and letting them go. Know that you made the best choice for yourself at the time with whatever information was available to you. It's the turning point you need for this release.

What types of men have you been historically attracted to? What personality traits did each one have? Were there similarities between any of them? Were you more attracted to the negative than the positive? Each of these answers not only sheds light on the past choices you made, but also illuminates the choices you make going forward. It is time to acknowledge what was working and what wasn't, and leave behind the choices you made that didn't bring you what you wanted.

If what you have been doing in the dating world currently is not working for you, there is only one option that is within your power that will work, and that option is to change your programmed mindset to be more in line with what you want the outcome to be.

Let's take a look at the difference between a lump of coal and a brilliant diamond. They are both are made from the same material, but the outcome is different depending on the pressure put on the material. The objective is to take those "coal" beliefs and change them to "diamond." You are perfect just the way you are; so let's just tweak your thoughts and mindset to reflect what you desire!

Relationship ABCs

There are three parts to developing a diamond mindset:

1. Assess where you are now—identify the present challenges in the areas which includes physical, emotional and spiritual issues;

2. Balance what you acknowledge to be the areas that aren't working by determining what you would

like to improve in your life. This not only applies to dating and relationships, but also family, spirituality, career, diet and exercise. Let's think of it as our bucket list chart.

3. Change what you determine is not working for you. Typically you pick one or two items from your bucket list chart and strategize the change plan over a two week period. Small steps take you farther and stick better than trying to make 100 changes at one time. This will take your newly energized mindset and manifest the positive changes so that it works for you and your relationship style.

I'm going to take you on a journey to discover your authentic self through a new understanding of how your body energy serves you. Although you can't see it, you can feel the changes happening as you move forward. You will discover what's been holding you back and learn to celebrate your beautiful spirit, bring it out of hiding, and let it out into the open to soar!

The W.I.S.E™ Method

This W.I.S.E™ Method, taught at the Institute of Healing Arts & Sciences (IHAS) was created by Dr. Dorothy Martin-Neville, the institute's founder. Dorothy began work in private practice as a psychotherapist in the 1980s. She also studied advanced acupressure, iridology, reflexology, Reiki, hypnotherapy, Jinn Shin Do, and Consecrate. She spent four years training with The Barbara Brennan School of Healing. Along the way, she developed a pattern of working that combined what she considered to be the best parts of every one of the above-listed modalities with her traditional psychotherapeutic training. Because she used an integrative approach in working with the whole person—emotionally, spiritually, physically, and energetically—she called her approach The

W.I.S.E.™ Method, standing for the Wholistic, Integrated, and Spiritual Energies of the body.

The W.I.S.E.™ Method works to support you in releasing energetic blocks that can weigh you down and keep you in survival mode instead of thriving. Fear, anger, abandonment, and loneliness can all be addressed, and the body feels the difference in the release. It will give you a new vision of relationship success, because you will be aware of what you need to work on at a deeper level, a level that will bring you what you want not only in relationships, but also in other areas of your life.

Learning to recognize when your body is out of balance, when there are pockets of tightness or weakness, allows you to course-correct and heal before the cost is too high, perhaps even before the problem is physical. Developing self-awareness is an exciting undertaking that allows the healing to be done by you, with assistance, in an environment of love and support and without judgment.

Beliefs and Behaviors

There are two areas in your life that we will concentrate on to give you a lasting and positive foundation going forward, and that is assessing your beliefs and behaviors. When you were growing up you were taught certain beliefs about the world from your parents, which was all you knew. One example would be that all Italians make great cooks, or that men are more successful in the workplace than women. Did your parents ever judge you based on one of their own beliefs they were taught? There might have been a time when you questioned a belief, as you began living in your own individual world. In order to make changes in your life it is necessary to "take inventory" of what those beliefs are, and if you still hold on to them today.

Your programmed behavior patterns are the second piece of the equation. Understanding how you react to situations, both positive and negative, will give you the insight to where you feel you need to shift in order to lead a happier and healthier life.

1. Beliefs—The Body's Energy Systems

There are many different kinds of energy systems, for instance, in science, engineering, and the human body. We will be talking about the body's energy system, or chakras.

Originating from Sanskrit, a chakra is an energy center in the body. There are seven chakras, and each serves a purpose, relating not only to an organ or specific part of the body, but also to emotional strengths and weaknesses. Each of us has strengths and deficiencies in certain areas, and it's helpful to know ourselves well enough to know where those are. Ideally, our energy system would always be in balance. When things start to become unbalanced or restricted, that's when disease, illness, and fear rear their ugly heads.

When people hold on to fears, those fears manifest in their cell tissue. As Carolyn Myss states in her book *Why People Don't Heal and How They Can*, "Your biography is your biology." Deeply rooted fears get in the way of not only your relationship choices but also your ability to think clearly.

Here are the seven chakras we will be covering in this book.

- ♦ First Chakra: The Root—Family & Security
- ♦ Second Chakra: The Sacral—Creativity & Sexuality
- ♦ Third Chakra: The Solar Plexus—Wisdom & Power
- ♦ Fourth Chakra: The Heart—Love & Healing
- ♦ Fifth Chakra: The Throat—Communication
- ♦ Sixth Chakra: The Third Eye—Intuition & Awareness
- ♦ Seventh Chakra: The Crown—Spirituality

Through exploring these chakras, you will learn how your beliefs and actions affect your outcomes, and you become aware of fears, anger, and self-defeating behaviors as well as your authentic beauty, which is sometimes hidden deep within some thought that you never knew you had. All of this self-analysis is beneficial, as everyone has the capacity for goodness. It's just that sometimes that goodness gets lost in beliefs that no longer serve you. Your willingness to explore the deeper, more meaningful pieces of what makes you a beautiful and desirable woman is exciting, and your newfound awareness will bring you happiness and success. Your energy will shine, and the outside world will open up and provide new opportunities for successful relationships.

2. Behaviors—Core Energetics™ Character Structures

There are many theories of the human personality, and the one that was taught by Dorothy at IHAS was an approach developed by John Pierrakos MD, a psychiatrist and colleague of Wilhelm Reich. He called this approach Core Energetics™. It includes five personality behavior types or "structures."

The character structures discussed in Core Energetics reflect both positive and negative aspects of characters. If we suffer from stress or fear, it is helpful to see which character structures define us. Once defined, we can shift the negative behavior into positive.

It is important to understand your dynamics to be able to temper yourself when you are feeling fearful, hurt, betrayed, lied to, and in how you view life in general.

Chapter 3
ASSESS YOUR BELIEFS

Assessing your current lifestyle in the areas of physical activity, relationships, career and spirituality is what is called Primary Foods at The Institute of Integrative Nutrition. It is important as a life coach to begin with these areas of your life. Living a happy and healthy life is not only about the food you eat, but it's also about other important areas of your life. The belief systems you have acquired throughout your life are a result of many things, including your family values, religious roots, childhood experiences, and others. Step one creates a baseline assessment of all of the belief systems you live by.

Even though your primary focus may be on dating and relationships, having a basic idea of the other areas is enlightening and helps bring awareness of other roadblocks that may have tied into your relationship experiences in the past.

The Seven Energy Centers
Are you aware that our body has seven energy centers that are l responsible for our various moods and behaviors?

Humans are prone to have terrible mood swings. At times we feel positive, and sometimes we feel low, there are times when we can concentrate better than other times. That is because the body's chakras are blocked or may be more active. Chakras are the energy centers in our body. Almost all religions have the concept of chakras in different ways.

Chakras control particular parts of the body, energizing their respective organs, and bring total harmony within the body. If any of the chakras are blocked, then energy cannot flow freely. Although you cannot see the chakras, you can feel them.

There are many explanations of energy systems, for instance, in science, exercise, engineering, and the human body. Let's take a look at each one, and see if there is anything that resonates with you. Having the knowledge of your energy flow will come into play later on in this book when we discuss relationships and dating, and what to look for in a man as far as strengths and compatibility.

First Chakra—The Root (Family & Security)

The first chakra is what keeps you rooted to the earth, or grounded. Similar to the foundation of a house which needs to be perfectly balanced for it to be stable, so the root chakra must be balanced and secure before all others. It is the foundation of our body's energy system. This chakra connects us to our physical world.

Our sense of security begins here. If you've ever experienced the "fight or flight" fear response, you know the feeling of first root chakra fear. When you have a traumatic experience, it affects this part of your body's energy flow.

To be resilient at this first level, you must develop a positive view of yourself and confidence in your strengths and abilities in the physical world. The fear of flying, fear of job loss, fear of losing money, or a fear of breaking away from the family are all associated with the root chakra.

First Chakra Basic Issues

1. Money

Our relationship with money affects the first chakra. Were you taught that spending money on yourself was selfish? Were you expected to save every penny you earned and buy clothing secondhand instead of new? Were you never taught how to make a budget, and so you find yourself with more month than money? Were you never taught how to balance your checkbook and find yourself always bouncing checks?

Having a healthy relationship with money is one of the major areas associated with the root chakra. If you lack the ability to have a healthy relationship with money, you will not have an opportunity to succeed in other areas of your life.

I see many clients who have a hard time parting with their money, especially if it means spending it on themselves. One of them, Cindy, loves to cook, and she also needed to lose about 20 pounds. A local culinary store had a three-hour organic cooking class in the evening, and Cindy was very interested. But when she found out the cost was $75, she declined. "That's too much money," she said. When I asked her what she usually spends when going out with her friends on a Friday night, she said $60.

What is Cindy's reasoning as to why she wouldn't want to invest in herself? She was brought up with the belief that unless you need it to pay expenses, spending money on yourself is selfish. She certainly could afford it, but somehow felt the money was not worth spending. My advice is: Invest in yourself!

2. Family

I grew up the second of four children in a typical middle-class family. My dad had a good job working in New York City, and my mom stayed home and raised us. We were blessed to live in a decent neighborhood with lots of kids.

I don't ever recall being raised with preconceived ideas about race or religion, as we had limited exposure to anyone different from ourselves. I do remember some of the things we were taught, like the man works and the woman stays home and tends to the children. Back then, the boys went to college and the girls got secretarial jobs, so my sisters and I were not encouraged to further our education after high school. We were taught that you never hit a woman, the man handles the money, and the woman gets an allowance. Think about some of the beliefs your family taught you. As you grew up, did some of them start to no longer make sense? Were you able to move past them? If so, congratulations, it's the first step toward a more independent mindset!

3. Religion

Structured religion plays a large part in the first chakra. There are many religions to choose from, and they all have their own set of rules for how we should conduct our lives. These rules may benefit the group, but they play a role in influencing our first chakra beliefs, and often they set limits that are unhelpful. For example, there may be a rule about donating a percentage of your income to a church or temple. Some ask members to take a vow of poverty and give up all of their worldly possessions. There may also be a belief that money is the root of all evil, and you may be told that if you give it to the religious organization you will be saved, but if you don't, you will burn in hell. At this point, people are being controlled by this fear. Some other examples of religious beliefs concern reproduction, for example, a rule prohibiting contraception or a belief that abortion is wrong.

Religious cults are notorious for drawing upon the first chakra fears and searching out vulnerable individuals who will "sell their souls" and become followers of the only truth toward salvation. A good example is Jim Jones, who led his followers to Jonestown only to end up presiding over and orchestrating mass suicide.

4. Communities

Many global communities remain in a "tribal" mindset, which constitutes the belief of following a group or government. It becomes unacceptable to try to break away to be more of an independent thinker. Some families have strong beliefs in how things should be in life, and many times as an individual comes into their own and tries to "break away" from family beliefs, they experience guilt, either on their own or from pressure of their family. For example, how many times have you heard something like, "All Italians are good cooks," or "Men who wear their ball caps backwards are not very bright," or "I always have trouble saving money, it runs in our family," or "I'll never succeed in life unless I go to college"? These are examples of societal beliefs without merit.

5. Relationships

Relationships in the first chakra have to do with everything mentioned above: relationships with groups, with family, and with money. Through these relationships, you form a solid foundation of how you believe the world should be.

If you have reached your 50s and you still have the beliefs you were taught as a child, you may still seek approval from your family (or grown children) for the relationship choices you make. Or you may find yourself choosing someone who reminds you of your father, even if he was abusive. You might choose someone like him because it's all you know. Maybe you were taught never to question authority, or that the man makes all the decisions. Can you see how your beliefs can influence your current relationship if you haven't moved past them?

When the Chakra Is out of Balance

You can make changes by observing where you may be held back by beliefs tied to family loyalty. You may be feeling fearful over your security or survival. Do you have money saved? Is your job secure?

If you are struggling in your relationship, especially with issues of trust, it will affect your overall health and well-being as fears and insecurities take root. Fortunately, this can be cleared, and you can shift your thoughts, beliefs, and actions so that you can experience the safety and security you deserve. It begins by acknowledging where your challenges lie.

Often, I find that my female clients who have challenges at the first chakra level never feel supported in their relationship. They feel that to get anything done right; they have to do it themselves. And so they go about their business in silence, building resentment that the other partner has no idea exists, when all they had to do was communicate.

Since your energy flows up from the ground, if your first chakra is blocked, it is limiting the flow of energy in your body and potentially impacting your health as well as success in relationships, with money, or in your career.

If your chakra is out of balance, you could experience a lack of energy or lack of confidence dealing with anything outside of your comfort zone. You may even develop eating disorders, adrenal fatigue, foot and leg pain, or colon, immune system, or bone disorders.

Self-Assessment Quiz

Please read the questions below and answer truthfully. If three or more are affirmative, your root chakra needs attention:

1. Do you suffer from any allergies?

2. Do you have any skin rashes?

3. Do you suffer from chronic yeast overgrowth?

4. Do you have difficulty achieving orgasm?

5. Do you have osteoporosis?

6. Do you feel aggressive?

7. Do you have overwhelming fears and feel unsafe?

8. Do you often feel there is not enough of something?

9. Do you ever feel like you have no control or choice? In what areas?

10. Do you have UTI or kidney issues?

11. Do you have trouble trusting people?

12. Are there healthy relationship boundaries in your life?

13. Do you hate change or fear instability?

Recommended Activities

Here are some activities you can do to support your first chakra that are considered "grounding" activities:

♦   Gardening

♦   Get a massage

♦ Drumming

♦ Running or jogging

♦ Take a nature walk

♦ Spend time at the beach

The section at the end of this chapter called Acknowledge and Growth will address techniques to help balance the first chakra.

Summary—The Root Chakra

The Root Chakra centers upon our core needs for survival, security and livelihood. When the Root Chakra is unbalanced, you will feel ungrounded, confused and lack the ability to move forward. Without a balanced Root Chakra, it is impossible to balance the other chakras fully.

Color

♦ Red

Body Organs Affected

♦ Spine

♦ Legs

♦ Bones

♦ Feet

♦ Rectum

♦ Prostate

♦ Immune system

Common Illnesses

♦ Addictions

♦ Anorexia

♦ Arthritis

- Constipation
- Crohn's disease
- Obesity

Signs of Balance

- Feeling grounded
- Secure
- Safe
- Content

Signs of Imbalance

- Ungrounded
- Fearful
- Insecure
- Unclear of purpose
- Confused

Second Chakra—The Sacral (Creativity & Sexuality)

Second Chakra

Creativity & Sexuality

The sacral chakra has to do with your sexuality and creativity. When this chakra is properly balanced, your emotional well-being is positive. The issues affected are creativity, sexuality, money, relationships, emotions, and intimacy. Creativity begins in this chakra. Passion fuels your creative energy in the areas of sexual relationships, friendships, business and financial partnerships, and power.

Second Chakra Basic Issues

1. Sexuality

The second chakra is considered the "pleasure seeker." Unlike the first chakra, which has relationships with groups, the second chakra focuses on one-on-one relationships. Emotions, intimacy, and warmth are among its associations, and your self-worth and self-image can either be healthy or unhealthy, depending on your life-experiences. As your relationships begin to provide positive or negative interactions, you begin to set beliefs about yourself based on those interactions.

It is important to note how your past relationships play into your current self-image. Did you date someone who always told you that you weren't good enough? Did they ever compliment you or give you positive feedback on your appearance? Were they gentle and kind, or rough and abrasive? Were you constantly second-guessing your choices because you relied on your partner to approve?

Many women feel guilty about their sexuality. They were taught that they needed to cover up or risk looking cheap and trampy. Any sign of sensuality was frowned upon, so it was common to try to be "invisible" to the world, as that was a very safe place to be. Any compliment was denied, as it was thought to be selfish and conceited.

2. Relationships

Relationships at the second chakra level are based primarily on lust or emotional neediness. This energy is how we begin to relate to others outside of the family, exploring new relationships and discovering the power of choice.

Every relationship we create has a purpose, no matter how painful, to help us become more aware of ourselves and our limitations.

Sexually, this is the pleasure chakra that "turns us on," and is deeply connected to our partnerships with others. Sexual eroticism is a form of physical and emotional freedom as well as spiritual liberation because it is about being in the moment so we can let go of our fears and boundaries to enjoy happiness.

When the Chakra Is out of Balance

When there is an imbalance in this area, sexual disorders, addictions, and other emotionally charged dysfunctions may occur. It is the passion and pleasure center. Intimacy is part of this chakra. This chakra is the storage center for all experiences associated with love and hate. When a woman encounters a sexual trauma, the second chakra's energy is literally "shut down."

If your second chakra is weak, you may be plagued by guilt and unwilling to forgive yourself for past mistakes. You may develop a fragile sense of self-worth, or become easily offended by the words or actions of others. You may develop any of the following health challenges: bowel disorders, bladder or urinary tract infections, or chronic lower back pain.

Self-Assessment Quiz

Please read the questions below and answer truthfully. If three or more are affirmative, your sacral chakra needs attention:

1. Do you have infertility issues?

2. Are you creative?

3. Do you suffer from cramps, PMS, or moodiness during your menstrual cycle?

4. How often do you do things that you don't enjoy? That you do enjoy?

5. When you do things for others, is it from a genuine desire to be of service to them or are you trying to win their approval?

6. Do you have low back pain or sciatica?

7. Do you have issues with money, fear there will not be enough, or trouble feeling worthy of the money you deserve?

8. Do you ever overindulge?

9. Do you suffer from adrenal burnout or fatigue?

10. Are you a jealous person?

11. Do you feel you have to struggle in life and that everything is hard?

12. Do you have co-dependent relationships? How do you contribute to them?

13. Do you have bouts of low self-esteem?

14. Do you often suffer from guilt that is hard to address?

15. Do you find it hard to be creative?

Recommended Activities

- Baths
- Massage
- Acupuncture
- Dance
- Swimming

♦ Yoga

♦ Creating art

The section at the end of this chapter called Acknowledge and Growth will address techniques to help balance the second chakra.

Summary—The Sacral Chakra

The Sacral Chakra influences personal creativity ranging from artistic expression to creative problem solving. Healthy sexual desire and expression are also controlled by the Sacral Chakra, though communicating sexual desires are also directly affected by the Throat Chakra.

Color

♦ Orange

Body Organs Affected

♦ Sexual organs

♦ Large intestine

♦ Lower vertebrae

♦ Pelvis

♦ Appendix

♦ Bladder

♦ Hip area

♦ Gonads

♦ Ovaries

Common Illnesses

♦ Impotence

♦ Uterine problems

♦ Eating disorders

♦ Gout

Signs of Balance

♦ Smooth creative flow

♦ Healthy sexual desire

♦ Positive outlook

Symptoms of Imbalance

♦ Sexual problems or dysfunction

♦ Fear of sexual or emotional intimacy

♦ Infidelity

♦ Needy or withdrawn

♦ Discomfort with gender roles

Third Chakra—The Solar Plexus (Wisdom & Power)

Your self-respect and personal power lie in this area. When balanced, you are "comfortable in your own skin" and tend to be more playful. This chakra relates to our relationship with ourselves. What beliefs do we hold about ourselves, our appearance, intelligence, physical abilities, and skills? Do we have low self-esteem?

This chakra is the center of personal strength, learning, and comprehension. You will begin to develop a strong sense of self and can set personal boundaries by building self-esteem and willpower.

When the Chakra Is out of Balance

When this chakra is out of balance, it affects your self-esteem and respect for others. There is a tendency toward depression, fear of rejection, oversensitivity to criticism, and indecisiveness. You may see yourself as powerless, and find ways of shaming yourself. You may experience digestive problems, ulcers, liver problems, gall stones, or pancreatic disorders such as diabetes or hypoglycemia.

Self-Assessment Quiz

Please read the questions below and answer truthfully. If three or more answers are affirmative, your third chakra needs attention:

1. Do you feel yourself being defensive or aggressive? If so, how does that serve you?

2. Do you struggle with self-control? In what areas do you struggle? Where do you exercise discipline?

3. Do you ever feel powerless? If so, when did this first begin?

4. Do you suffer from digestive issues, constipation, or gas?

5. Do you have weight issues?

6. Do you suffer from addictions?

7. Do you have diabetes?

8. Do you have ulcers?

9. Do you have gallbladder pain or stones?

10. Do you have fibromyalgia?

11. Do you have trouble sensing and accepting your gut instincts?

12. Do you feel like you jump into "warrior mode" if threatened?

13. Do you often feel under-appreciated?

14. Do you often volunteer to help others without being asked?

Recommended Activities

♦   Cycling

♦   Hiking

♦   Leadership roles

♦   Photography

♦   Solitude

The section at the end of this chapter called Acknowledge and Growth will address techniques to help balance the third chakra.

Summary—The Solar Plexus Chakra

The Solar Plexus Chakra strongly influences your identity and sense of self-worth. Imbalances can take on polar opposites ranging from low self-esteem to arrogant and selfish behavior.

Color

♦   Yellow

Body Organs Affected

♦   Abdomen

♦   Upper intestines

♦ Liver

♦ Gallbladder

♦ Kidneys

♦ Pancreas

♦ Adrenal glands

♦ Spleen

Common Illnesses

♦ Ulcers

♦ Diabetes

♦ Hepatitis

♦ Hypoglycemia

♦ Constipation

Signs of Balance

♦ Comfortable in own skin

♦ Inner Peace

♦ Confidence without arrogance

♦ Calm demeanor

♦ Patient

♦ Flexible

Symptoms of Imbalance

♦ Egotistical behavior

♦ Feeling abandoned or rejected

♦ Feeling the world revolves around you

♦ Low self-esteem

♦ Arrogance

♦ Difficulty understanding or controlling emotions

- ◆ Rebellious
- ◆ Too eager to please
- ◆ Nervous or stressed out
- ◆ Addictive behavior including eating disorders

Fourth Chakra—The Heart (Love & Healing)

The heart chakra has to do with one's ability to love and accept love from others. When the heart chakra is balanced, you show compassion. When the chakra is unbalanced, it is hard to give or receive love, as the heart is closed to the outside world.

If there is an emotional trauma to the heart such as a relationship breakup or the death of a child, the energy in the heart is blocked or constricted. Sometimes people in these circumstances can develop diseases such as breast cancer or a heart attack because there is no healing energy flowing through the heart area. Although there is no medical connection, the heart energy is one of the most important areas of life, as our heart is the center of our life.

When the Chakra Is out of Balance

When the heart chakra is not balanced, there is a tendency toward excessive manipulation of emotions. Relationships can be ruined because there is a tendency to feel unloved, inferior, rejected, or lonely. You can become clingy and needy.

Self-Assessment Quiz

Please read the questions below and answer truthfully. If three or more are affirmative, your fourth chakra needs attention:

1. Do you have trouble nurturing yourself?

2. Do you have any breast tenderness?

3. Do you have heart or circulation issues?

4. Do you suffer from bronchitis or pneumonia?

5. Do you have difficulty feeling self-love?

6. Are you able to be open and honest about your feelings with another person?

7. Do you have trouble with your relationship intuition?

8. Do you put up walls in your relationships?

9. Do you have trouble nurturing yourself?

10. Do you have self-respect for yourself or others?

11. Are you able to forgive yourself and others?

12. Have you been a victim of abuse from a loved one?

13. Do you crave attention?

14. Are you able to receive gifts or appreciation from others?

Recommended Activities

♦ Spending time with family and pets

♦ Reiki

♦ Dance

♦ Massage

♦ Healing past relationships

♦ Letting go

The section at the end of this chapter called Acknowledge and Growth will address techniques to help balance the fourth chakra.

Summary—The Heart Chakra

The Heart Chakra influences the ability to give and receive love in a healthy way. The Heart Chakra also influences our ability to cope with the sadness of betrayals of a loved one or losing a loved one due to breakup, abandonment or death.

Color
♦ Green

Body Organs Affected
♦ Lungs

♦ Heart

♦ Bronchia

♦ Arms and hands

♦ Muscles

♦ Thymus gland

Common Illnesses
♦ Hypertension

♦ Emphysema

♦ Heart problems and chest pain

♦ Breast cancer

Signs of Balance
♦ Able to express love

♦ Giving

♦ Compassionate

♦ Joyful

Symptoms of Imbalance

♦ Unable to give or receive unconditional love

♦ Selfish

♦ Jealous

♦ Hateful

♦ Grief stricken

♦ Excessive loneliness

♦ Depression

♦ Feelings of alienation

Fifth Chakra—The Throat (Communication)

The throat chakra is the communication center where we voice our opinions and beliefs to the outside world, and also speak the truth to ourselves. Learning to express ourselves verbally is an important energy balance for our lives. This chakra serves as the mediator between thought and emotion and is the chakra that is commonly blocked.

Sometimes when people are susceptible to sore throats, I ask them, "What is it that you are not saying"? It's interesting to hear most people answer that they haven't said something or expressed themselves.

The choices we make have consequences on our health; even choosing to repress our anger may cause us to develop laryngitis.

If you have ever experienced a "lump" in your throat, it usually means you may be having trouble speaking up or finding the right words to say.

It is important to have a healthy fifth chakra by expressing ourselves in the most truthful way possible. When this happens, we can speak our minds without forgetting our hearts.

It is rare that an individual is not carrying some tension in the neck, shoulders, or jaw. We were taught when we were younger, "If you don't have anything nice to say, don't say anything at all" or, "Children should be seen and not heard." Although there is some truth to both statements, the intention was to teach us how to speak and act in socially acceptable ways, not to shut us down.

The tension in the throat chakra is almost always the result of unspoken or non-expression of the truth. Have you ever said something that no one hears, only to have your words repeated by someone else and acknowledged as their own?

When the Chakra Is out of Balance

If your throat chakra is unbalanced, you may stop yourself from asking for what you want or have a problem speaking up. There is often a need to impress others and seek approval. You may experience the following health issues (on a frequent basis): sore throats, swollen glands in the neck/jaw, TMJ, sinus problems, and thyroid disorders.

Self-Assessment Quiz

Please read the questions below and answer truthfully. If three or more are affirmative, your fifth chakra needs attention:

1. Do you have thyroid issues?

2. Do you love to gossip?

3. Do you have trouble keeping a secret?

4. Do you get tension headaches often?

5. Do you overeat frequently?

6. Is your metabolism sluggish?

7. Do you suffer from laryngitis or frequent sore throats?

8. Do you grind your teeth at night?

9. Do you have dental issues?

10. Do you tend to ignore the messages your body is sending you?

11. Do you worry about what people will think if you speak up?

12. Were you creative as a child?

13. Are you always feeling rushed like there is never enough time?

Recommended Activities

♦ Hum, whistle or sing

♦ Play a musical instrument

♦ Journal

♦ Fasting

♦ Silence

♦ Retreats

The section at the end of this chapter called Acknowledge and Growth will address techniques to help balance the fifth chakra.

Summary—The Throat Chakra

The Throat Chakra strongly influences our ability to communicate our thoughts, opinions, desires and feelings, and our ability to hear, listen and understand others in our daily lives. The throat chakra also influences body language and written communication methods.

Color
♦ Blue

Body Organs Affected
♦ Vocals

♦ Mouth (jaw, teeth, gums and tongue)

♦ Neck and shoulders

♦ Thyroid and parathyroid glands

Common Illnesses
♦ Bronchitis

♦ Mouth ulcers

♦ Sore throat

Signs of Balance
♦ Effective Communication Skills

♦ Expressive

♦ Good Listener

♦ Patient

♦ Honest

♦ Receptive to criticism

Symptoms of Imbalance

♦ Poor communication skills

♦ Afraid to speak up

♦ Represses feelings

♦ Uncontrolled verbal outbursts

♦ Deceitful

♦ Manipulative

♦ Unable to listen

Sixth Chakra—The Third Eye (Intuition & Awareness)

The third eye chakra is our intuitive chakra, and connects to our sharp "sixth sense." This chakra gives us the ability to receive intuitive messages without cluttered thoughts; if the chakra is balanced, you learn to listen and trust those messages.

The third eye chakra influences the areas of our mind that control our common sense, wisdom, intelligence, memory retention, dreams, spirituality, and intuition.

A well-balanced chakra helps you dream of possibilities of what could be, while you are still conscious of reality.

When the Chakra Is out of Balance

An imbalanced chakra creates a fantasy, a nonexistent reality that is an escape from real life. Often you will lose your sense of purpose in life. You may experience headaches, sinus infections, or neurological disorders.

Self-Assessment Quiz

Please read the questions below and answer truthfully. If three or more are affirmative, your sixth chakra needs attention:

1. Do you suffer from migraines?

2. Do you suffer from depression or anxiety?

3. Do you have ear or eye issues?

4. Do you have trouble sleeping?

5. Do you have a poor memory?

6. Do you have trouble visualizing things?

7. Do you feel competitive?

8. Do you feel uneasy in a crowd?

9. Do you over-analyze things?

10. When you feel empathy, does it affect your mood? Are you affected by other people's moods?

Recommended Activities

♦   Finding wisdom in life's lessons and pain
♦   Tai Chi
♦   Qigong
♦   Contemplation
♦   Meditation
♦   Visualization
♦   Reading

♦ Letting go of old thought patterns

♦ Freedom

The section in this chapter called Acknowledge and Growth will address techniques to help balance the sixth chakra.

Summary—Third Eye Chakra

The Third Eye Chakra influences the areas of our mind that control our common sense, wisdom, intelligence, memory retention, dreams, spirituality and intuition.

Color

♦ Indigo or Deep Blue

Body Organs Affected

♦ Eyes

♦ Nose

♦ Ears

♦ Sinuses

♦ Forebrain

♦ Pituitary gland

Common Illnesses

♦ Blindness

♦ Brain tumor

♦ Cataracts

♦ Deafness

♦ Dyslexia

Signs of Balance

♦ Fast learner

♦ Clear memory

- ♦ Intelligent
- ♦ Sense of spirituality

Symptoms of Imbalance

- ♦ Non-sympathetic/Empathetic
- ♦ Judgmental
- ♦ Over-intellectualizing
- ♦ Lacks common sense
- ♦ Forgetful
- ♦ Sleep/dream/nightmare issues

Seventh Chakra—The Crown (Spirituality)

Seventh Chakra
Spirituality

The crown chakra is the closest chakra to the heavens, also known as the "spiritual chakra." Many humans never develop a balance in this chakra. It is on the top of the head and is associated with the brain and the entire nervous system.

Just as the root chakra connects us to the earth, the crown chakra connects us to the heavens. It is the chakra of dreamers and true spirituality.

From a Chinese perspective, the top of the head is the receptor of "sky," or yang energy. This chakra is seen as the funnel into which the "higher" thoughts are poured. This chakra's connection to a higher power is shown in most religious pictures as a halo above the head. It is the gateway that connects us both to the physical and non-physical realms of our existence.

When a Chakra Is out of Balance

If your seventh chakra is weak, you may feel disconnected to the spiritual world, and feelings of abandonment may surface. You may experience anxiety, depression, migraines, amnesia, ADD, or dyslexia.

Self-Assessment Quiz

Please read the questions below and answer truthfully. If three or more are affirmative, your seventh chakra needs attention:

1. Do you have any genetic disorders?

2. Do you have any life-threatening illnesses?

3. Do you have any learning disabilities?

4. Do you have a short attention span?

5. Do you have any seizure disorders?

6. Do you feel light-headed or dizzy often?

7. Do you feel hurt when criticized?

8. Do you feel separate from God?

Recommended Activities

- ♦ Make joy and happiness a priority
- ♦ Take naps
- ♦ Laugh
- ♦ Funny movies and books
- ♦ Prayer or reading scripture
- ♦ Astrology

The section at the end of this chapter called Acknowledge and Growth will address techniques to help balance the seventh chakra.

Summary—The Crown Chakra

The Crown Chakra influences our deeper understanding of ourselves beyond the physical or material.

Color

♦ Violet

Body Organs Affected

♦ Central nervous system

♦ Skull and cerebral cortex

♦ Pineal gland

Common Illnesses

♦ Alzheimer's

♦ Depression

♦ Dizziness

♦ Epilepsy

♦ Multiple sclerosis

Signs of Balance

♦ Balanced spiritual life

♦ Feels that life has purpose

♦ Feels a connection with others

♦ Wise

♦ Insightful

Symptoms of Imbalance

- ◆ Unspiritual
- ◆ Excessive fear of death
- ◆ Feeling alone in the universe
- ◆ Having a God-Complex
- ◆ Feeling unloved by or angry at God
- ◆ Depression

Acknowledgment and Growth

After taking the chakra self-assessment quizzes, you should have a clearer idea of where you may need work to balance the chakras. Ideally, there should be a healthy flow of energy from your feet to the top of your head. Wherever your imbalances lie, if you are honest with yourself and you are ready to make changes, you will be pleasantly surprised how quickly you can improve the world around you.

Each chakra has a color associated with it, starting with red and going all the way to violet. This beautiful rainbow of energy begins with the heaviest vibrations (root chakra) and ends up with the lightest (crown chakra), as your energy progresses from being grounded to enlightened.

Jim is a man who works as a Reiki practitioner and does past life readings. He is highly intuitive and loves to dance. Jim also is accident-prone and can't seem to keep his finances in order, frequently bouncing checks. Does Jim appear to be grounded and present? The obvious answer is no. That doesn't mean he is unhappy. But if Jim were to ask me what he needs to do to become more responsible with his money, I would recommend that he work on his first chakra grounding technique.

The Grounding Technique

Here is a simple grounding technique you can use anytime you feel anxious or depressed. Sitting in a chair:

♦ Plant your feet on the ground. Place both feet flat on the ground. Sit up straight, feeling the chair support you. Feel your feet touch the floor.

♦ Breathe. Inhale slowly while mentally counting to five. Then exhale completely to the count of five. Repeat five times.

♦ Notice what you see around you. Say out loud five things you see, four things you hear, three things you can feel, and two things you smell.

Here are some other grounding techniques you can try:

♦ Bring your attention to your feet. Curl your toes and hold for a few minutes. Release and push down on your heels. Repeat as needed

♦ Grab tightly to something like the top of a chair. Hold it as tight as you can while you focus on breathing slowly. Release and repeat as you need to.

♦ Stand with your back against a wall or counter. Focus on breathing slowly.

Tips for Grounding

When doing any grounding technique, make sure to keep your eyes open so that you can see and focus on what is around you at that moment. It is also a good idea to speak out loud, describing what you are seeing and doing.

Like any other skill, it is important to practice grounding techniques. It's helpful to try doing them when you are calm and to and practice often, so that when you need to use them, you already know how to do it.

The Benefits of Grounding

When you practice grounding, there are many benefits to your well-being. You will feel more relaxed, more alert, and more mindful of your surroundings. You will also find you have better concentration. Grounding techniques are one of the best things you can do to balance your chakras and become more present.

Chapter 4
BEHAVIOR ASSESSMENT

Before you can even begin to understand what to focus on, you first need to identify your authentic personality characteristics. There are many theories of the human personality. This book references The Core Energetics™ program developed years ago by John Pierrakos, MD, who was trained under Wilhelm Reich. William Reich was a student of Sigmund Freud, and he introduced the notion and science of "characterology" along with its five basic character types. Each character has a set of bodily postures, muscular skeletal structuring, touch, feeling, and contact presentations to the world, plus a mask or manner of presenting a false appearance to the world. Core Energetics has been a fundamental part of modern psychiatry and has helped countless people understand how they react to situations in both a healthy and unhealthy way.

Pierrakos founded the Institute of Core Energetics in 1973 in New York City. Currently, the Institute offers a four-year program for practitioners to specialize in the Core Energetics program. Pierrakos passed away on February 1, 2011, a few days before his eightieth birthday and after a long journey teaching Core Energetics in the US, Australia, Brazil, Mexico, Holland, Germany, Italy, and France. He was a brilliant man with the courage to be transparent as a human being and a leader.

The character structures discussed in Core Energetics reflect both positive and negative aspects of our personalities. If we suffer from stress or fear, it is helpful to be able to see which type of character behaviors define us. Once defined, we have the opportunity to change any unhealthy behaviors into healthy ones through awareness and a mindset shift.

You can spend years studying every detail of each of the character structures. For the purpose of this book, I will include the most relevant parts and try to keep it interesting and entertaining. It is important to understand your dynamics to be able to temper yourself when you are fearful or hurt, feel betrayed or lied to, or consider how you view life in general. In looking at the personality descriptions in this chapter, you will see they all have different strengths and weaknesses. We may describe ourselves with just one type or many. Each type has both healthy and unhealthy attributes, positive and excessive traits. Not only will you understand yourself better, but you will be able to decide what kind of personality behavior you are looking for in a man.

Why We Need to Know This

To improve our lives and the way we see the world, we need to recognize what exists, or as they say *"you can't change what you don't acknowledge."* There are five different approaches to viewing a situation, and knowing which one you identify with will help you understand which personality behavior defines you.

In this chapter you will start to understand the strengths and weaknesses of each of the character structures and identify with one or two. We will review techniques on how to move from unhealthy behavior to heathy in the Balance chapter.

The Five Personality Types

Creative/Schizoid (The Creator)

The Creator has a knack for figuring things out. Mental faculties are usually highly developed; Creators are intellectuals. Gut feelings are not something they put emphasis on, and they do not trust instinctive response when it comes up. Speech and writing can be exact, partly because they don't believe others will understand them without reading what they write.

Their object is to be able to work long stretches without boredom or a break. They may work to the point of exhaustion. They work well without supervision, and are often highly valued in the workplace. They do well with technology, but sometimes have trouble dealing with social situations. Suspicion and distrust are usually part of their relationship pattern, and they are sometimes reluctant to get involved more than superficially. They tend to become isolated out of a need to be alone because they don't trust. They sense hostility in others quickly, and are not wired to see the positive first.

Creators sometimes have difficulty being noticed in the workplace, which may result in employers not seeing them and possibly passing them over for promotions. Much of the time, they aren't "present" enough to be valued, and they find it hard to connect on a deeper emotional level with other people because they intellectualize everything. In their healthy state, they are sensitive and perceptive. They are brilliant, innovative thinkers, and imaginative, creative artists.

Physical Characteristics

Usually, the body is narrowed and tense. There is stiffness to their movement, it does not look natural. The arms hang like appendages rather than extensions of the body. The Creative often has hammer toes and a raised arch in the feet. The feet may be larger than the ankles, be cold to the touch, have gnarled toes, and poor circulation. They appear ungrounded and may walk awkwardly. They often have trouble with balance.

Common illnesses include sciatica, knee problems, bone disorders, anxiety, and persistent fears.

Relationships

Johnny is a computer programmer who spends most of his free time playing video games at home. He doesn't have much of a social life, and at age 54, most of his peers are married. When he attends work functions, he doesn't interact one-on-one, but hangs out with whoever is nearest to the bar.

Johnny recently met a woman at work when she struck up a conversation on the elevator. Sarah works in a different company on the floor below, and they both have an interest in social media and current events. They ran into each other shortly after that in the building's cafeteria and sat together for lunch. Sarah is an outgoing talker, and asked Johnny if he would like to go out for happy hour on Friday night to the café down the block. Johnny got nervous and declined, saying he had to go out of town that Friday evening, but he thanked Sarah. He was interested in her, but was afraid he would eventually get rejected, as had happened with so many women before.

Should Johnny have said yes? Was he embarrassed that he didn't make the first move? Did he even know how to ask a woman out?

As you can see, Johnny has a typical Schizoid behavior, and as he became fearful, he pulled away from what could have been an excellent start to a relationship. Did Johnny miss the signals Sarah sent that she was interested? Will Johnny realize that he was given an opportunity and missed it? One will never know, but this is common for those who have Schizoid personality behavior.

The Schizoid at some point may enter into an abusive relationship with a partner who has unresolved anger issues. They often live alone for long periods of time because they do not know how to initiate relationships. They usually have difficulty ending a relationship without a strong, compelling reason.

The Creator does not always connect emotionally to their partner and may have additional sexual partners who are chosen because they are available, not necessarily because they are attractive. In a monogamous relationship, sex may be frequent, but mechanical and without emotion.

It is common for the Creator to withdrawal from a situation before it gets complicated, and they may want to leave their partner instead of trying to resolve the issue. This happens because they do not like conflict. It is difficult for them to stay grounded, so when things become challenging, they "check out."

Famous Actors/Characters

Characters such as Phoebe from *Friends*, Kramer from *Seinfeld* and the Scarecrow from *The Wizard of Oz* demonstrate the characteristics of this structure. Others, such as Albert Einstein, Gandhi and Stephen Hawking personify the strengths, creativity, and ability to think outside of the box.

Creative/Schizoid Checklist

Check off all that apply:

Healthy Behavior

❏ Sensitive
❏ Perceptive

❏ Imaginative

❏ Spiritual

Unhealthy Behavior

❏ Persistent anxiety

❏ Not present

❏ Detached

Relationship Style

❏ Non-invasive

❏ Non-confrontational

❏ Suspicious

❏ Emotionally vulnerable

Common Illnesses

❏ Sciatica

❏ Knee problems

❏ Bone disorders

❏ Frequent illness in general

❏ Anxiety, frequent fears

❏ Inability to focus

❏ "Spaciness"

❏ Inability to be still

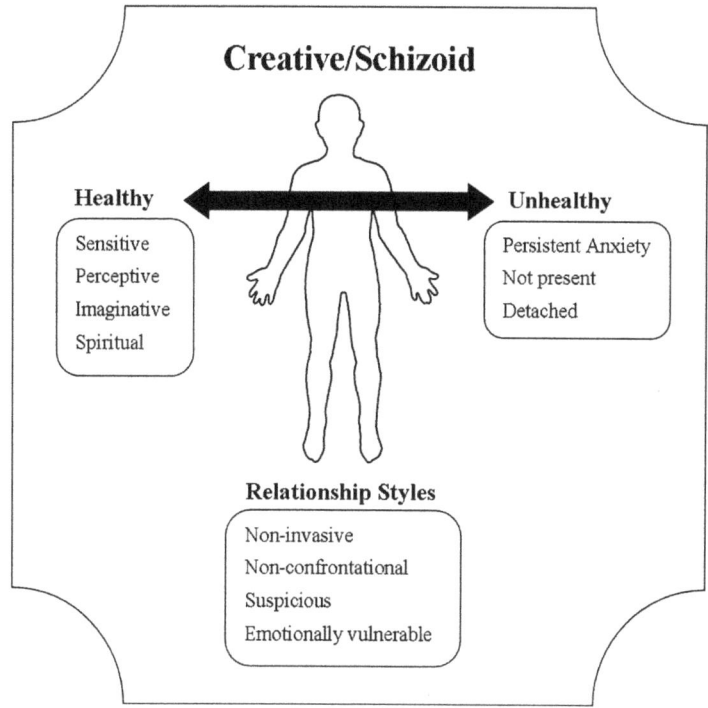

Creative/Schizoid

Healthy

Sensitive
Perceptive
Imaginative
Spiritual

Unhealthy

Persistent Anxiety
Not present
Detached

Relationship Styles

Non-invasive
Non-confrontational
Suspicious
Emotionally vulnerable

Empathetic/Oral (The Communicator)

The Oral personality has a genuine interest in others and is often found volunteering and giving of their time to help others. They easily express their feelings, except for anger. Socialization is a big part of who they are, they love being around people and having long conversations. They have an immense capacity to care deeply about the world, people, animals, and the environment through the gift of empathy and compassion. They easily relate to people who feel insecure, imperfect, lost, and hopeless because they often feel this way, too. Typical professions include human resources, health care workers, mothers, and others in a volunteer capacity.

This character structure is sometimes "undercharged," and frequently looks to feed off the energy of others. They make plans and start many projects that are beyond their capacity to finish. They take on too much responsibility, which soon begins to drain them, leading to collapse. They hold onto the belief that it is still "someone else's job to take care of them." They resent being responsible for themselves and their own needs.

They too often need someone else's energy to fill them up and desperately want to feel full all the time. This need for others to verify their self-worth can dominate their life and prevent them from creating positive change. This personality type can find itself involved with addictions.

Whenever the Empathetic person finds self-gratification, they feel immense guilt and feel they "do not deserve it." They may try to sabotage others' genuine attempts to help them. They can suffer from both depression and recurring minor physical illnesses, as their immune system are often suppressed. They often have poor diets.

The Empathetic person often has a social mask of being an "unconditional giver" or "martyr." Empathetic/Orals are deeply concerned with justice and fairness. They resent the inequity of the social system. They often champion the cause of underdogs and minorities. This resentment comes from feeling deprived. They are also not aggressive by nature. Mentally, they are intuitive and intellectual, but creative ideas are not put into action.

Orals usually like physical activity and sports that require endurance or graceful movement. They may take up sports such as marathons or bicycling.

Empathetic/Orals are often intellectuals, and they love conversation and also the written word. Talking is the way they try to connect to others, and long talks are preferred. They are often terrible listeners, however, because their "ear" is tuned to hear how other people's statements fit into their point of view. They often speak regarding right and wrong; Rules are seen as very important because they don't believe that expressing wants on their behalf will be well-received.

Empathetic/Orals hook into another's energy field to suck their energy and to fill themselves up. This is evident if you've ever been around someone who you feel is "sucking the life out of you." It can feel exhausting at times!

In their healthy state, they have the capacity to give to others in a deeply nurturing, truly healing way. They have an appreciation for the vastly abundant nature of existence and the joy of sharing. They are masters of connection between humans and animals. They are "heart-centered," and able, with practice, to radiate love and nurturance, generosity and abundance.

Physical Characteristics

In some Empathetic/Orals, their body looks malnourished, resembling someone who needs to eat more. They have a strong body where veins, muscles, and bones are prominent. In others, there may be a fat layer around the middle. This is not thick musculature, but rather a kind of "baby fat."

Their eyes have a longing, pleading look; their shoulders are rolled forward, collapsing the chest and sometimes causing shallow breathing.

Their body is often in pain, with frequent injuries or illnesses (lower back, knees, respiratory) that take a long time to heal. They also are prone to digestive disorders, Crohn's disease, irritable bowel syndrome, depression, chronic fatigue, addictions, and chronic mood swings. Recovering from illness or injuries is usually slow. The "sick" role may become an acceptable way to act out dependency and hostility, and the lifestyle may become structured around medical care.

Relationships

Because they need other peoples' energy to fill them up, people who tend to be co-dependent or caretakers are more likely to include the Empathetic/Oral in their life. This can lead to lovers eventually becoming resentful and angry because of how much they have given them.

They can be an energetic "bottomless pit," and often drive away partners who feel suffocated by their neediness and demands that never cease. They are often unable to sustain relationships after a brief period of intense involvement

Trying to get love and support is the motivation for them in relationships, and is often attempted through insistent care-giving. Relationship dynamics will go back and forth between intense "lost-in-love" involvement to abrupt endings as their struggles are acted out. Separation anxiety can be extreme, and Empathetic/Orals can hold on strongly to unsatisfying situations with lots of complaining.

They prefer childlike holding to adult sexual intimacy, and often do not find sex satisfying. Slow, tender movements are preferred to strong, passionate ones.

Famous Actors/Characters

Television and movie characters who portray this structure in their roles are Jake from *Two and a Half Men*, George from *Seinfeld*, and Ross from *Friends*. Oprah is an example of one who comes from the strength of this character structure, as she nurtures and fills the needs of others.

Empathetic/Oral Checklist

Check off all that apply:

Healthy Behavior

❑ Interested in others

❑ Empathic

❑ Easy to trust

❑ Non-threatening

❑ Tuned in to others' needs

❑ Expresses feelings easily, except anger

❑ Loyal

❑ Nurturing

❑ Capable of great love

Unhealthy Behavior

❑ Expect others to fill their needs

❑ Often don't know what they want

❑ Sense of entitlement

Relationship Style

❑ Can be empathetic and understanding

❑ Very joyful, with easy laughter

❑ Can be compassionate community builders

❑ Jealous

❑ Low energy investment

❑ Want to be taken care of

Common Illnesses

❑ Addictions

❑ Emotional instability or numbness

- ❏ Low immune system
- ❏ Reproductive issues
- ❏ Spleen or urinary tract problems
- ❏ Lower back problems
- ❏ Obesity
- ❏ Anorexia
- ❏ Bulimia

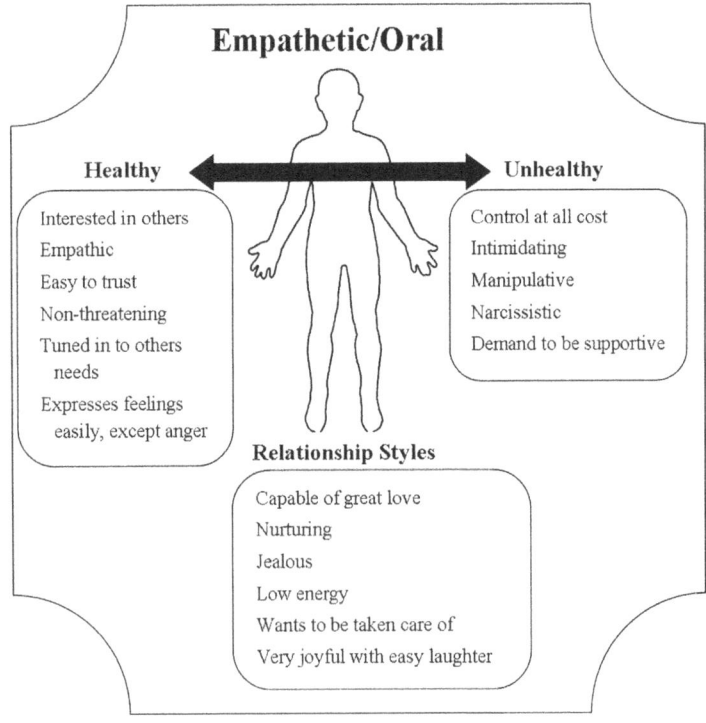

Empathetic/Oral

Healthy ⟷ **Unhealthy**

Interested in others
Empathic
Easy to trust
Non-threatening
Tuned in to others needs
Expresses feelings easily, except anger

Control at all cost
Intimidating
Manipulative
Narcissistic
Demand to be supportive

Relationship Styles

Capable of great love
Nurturing
Jealous
Low energy
Wants to be taken care of
Very joyful with easy laughter

Nurturer/Masochist (The Endurer)

The Nurturer often has a need to whine and complain. Anyone who tries to help will be frustrated by their helplessness, which is passive-aggressive and expressed in acts like being late, forgetting, or not answering a question. The absence of trust in others promotes helplessness. To the Nurturer, trust invites humiliation in their world.

The Endurer has a mind and style that is slower, duller, and less imaginative than most. They may suffer chronic low-grade depression due to the repression of their rage and anger. They are often identified at work as the "helper" to a higher authority figure, who may also abuse or control them.

They often lack spontaneity and can endure pain well. They also have enormous strength and energy, yet the stagnation of their energy sometimes brings fatigue.

In their healthy state, they care about others and are selfless. They are gifted mediators, compassionate, dependable, playful, hardworking, loyal, and capable of great love.

Physical Characteristics

The Endurer will often have a thick trunk and thick arms and legs. The muscles are tight. There is often a "cut-off bottom" in the buttocks. If you look at a scolded dog, when they put their tail between their legs, you can see this same cut-off effect. The neck is thick and short. The facial muscles are often tight, and the eyes either are small and beady, or they can be vacant. They have a high threshold for pain. Their body moves as a total unit, a rigid dense mass which has lost a lot of its flexibility.

Common diseases include digestive and eating disorders, ulcers, liver problems, excessive weight around the middle, muscle spasms, low energy, and chronic fatigue.

Relationships

In relationships, the Nurturer can feel close and give and receive some warmth, but the relationship can still exhibit a feeling of tension and pressure. This is attempted either through passive or self-damaging behavior or constant whining and complaining.

The Nurturer has a high sexual drive. Commonly there is a fascination with pornography.

Famous Actors/Characters

Characters in entertainment who demonstrate this structure are Chandler from *Friends*, Ray's mom on *Everybody Loves Raymond*, the Lion in *The Wizard of Oz*, and Rodney Dangerfield. Figures that represent the healthy component include Mother Theresa and Nelson Mandela.

Nurturer/Masochist Checklist

Check off all that apply:

Healthy Behavior

- ❏ Reliable
- ❏ Hard working
- ❏ Persevering
- ❏ Loyal
- ❏ Nurturing
- ❏ Capable of great love

Unhealthy Behavior

- ❏ Afraid to take risks
- ❏ Passive/aggressive
- ❏ Views self as weak
- ❏ Co-dependent

Relationship Style

- ❏ Very supportive
- ❏ Makes sacrifices easily
- ❏ Very affectionate and loving

❏ Passive-aggressive
❏ Feels victimized and overwhelmed frequently

Common Illnesses
❏ Digestive disorders
❏ Eating disorders
❏ Ulcers
❏ Liver problems
❏ Excessive weight around middle
❏ Muscle spasms and disorders
❏ Low energy
❏ Chronic fatigue

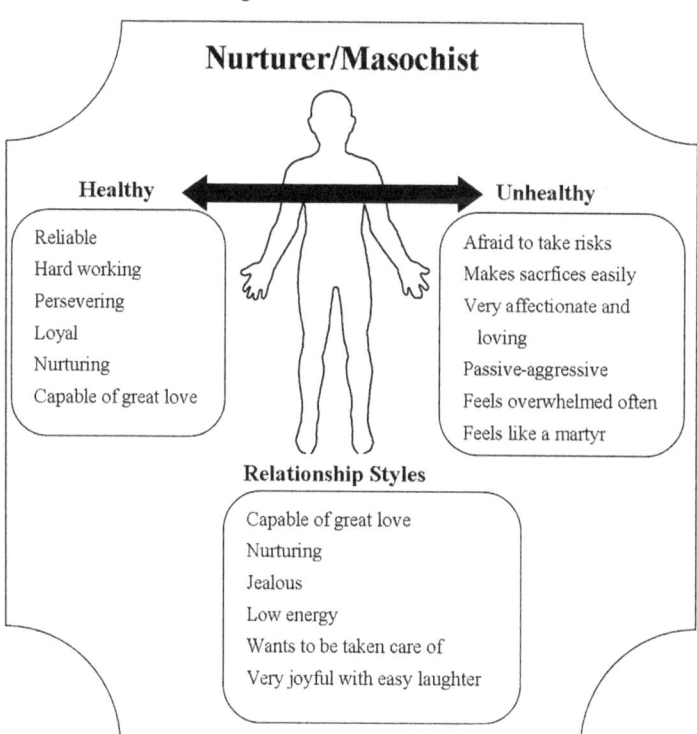

Nurturer/Masochist

Healthy

Reliable
Hard working
Persevering
Loyal
Nurturing
Capable of great love

Unhealthy

Afraid to take risks
Makes sacrfices easily
Very affectionate and
  loving
Passive-aggressive
Feels overwhelmed often
Feels like a martyr

Relationship Styles

Capable of great love
Nurturing
Jealous
Low energy
Wants to be taken care of
Very joyful with easy laughter

Leader/Psychopath (The Controller)

This person needs to be always moving, unable to relax or be still unless self-medicating with an addiction, or on the go. They are often seductive at first, then become controlling, especially when in a relationship. Over time, they may start to have trust issues with people. Paranoia creeps in, and they become aggressive and controlling.

They seek power and status and they will compete with others for it, but they often lack a certain moral fiber, and so will resort to manipulation to get what they want. In their healthy form, this personality is a natural leader who is charismatic and fearless and who can sum up people and situations with accuracy. They are intelligent, and can start and finish projects as well as inspire others to do the same. In relationships, they take charge of planning activities with ease. They are creative, perceptive, generous, and productive in positions of power. They are charismatic, bright, entertaining, charming, and eloquent.

Physical Characteristics

Their energy is held in the upper half of the body, especially in the head and shoulders. Their eyes are tense and controlling. They often look like they are "puffed up," as if they are holding their breath.

Common illnesses are stress-related muscle spasms, high blood pressure, gallbladder disorders, stroke, and heart attacks.

Relationships

The Leader's need to have "followers" is essential for this personality. It is through the "needing to be needed" that they maintain their feeling of power. They always have at least one follower, which will usually be a relationship partner. They will often have more than one partner, to prove potency and to prove he or she is not controlled by their partner.

They often "divide and conquer" to gain control of others, pitting people against each other, and then take the role of mediator or peacemaker.

Sex is often used to gain power, not pleasure, or to express revenge feelings. In a competitive corporate environment, they might thrive, but if they take the same approach in their relationships, they could create an unsafe and aggressive home environment.

Famous Actors/Characters

Actors such as Matthew McConaughey, Tom Selleck, George Clooney, and Al Pacino often portray the defensive component of this structure, as does Glenn Close as Alex Forrest in *Fatal Attraction*. Healthy leadership models include Martin Luther King and John F. Kennedy.

Leader/Psychopath Checklist

Check off all that apply:

Healthy Behavior

❏ Good leaders

❏ Charismatic

❏ Powerful Speakers

❏ Creative

❏ Generous

❏ Entertaining

Unhealthy Behavior

❏ Control at all costs

❏ Intimidating

❏ Manipulative

❏ Narcissistic

❏ Demanding to be supported

Relationship Style

- ❏ Adventurous
- ❏ Outgoing
- ❏ Protective
- ❏ Strong willed
- ❏ Forceful
- ❏ Limited time for intimacy

Common Illnesses

- ❏ Stress related muscle spasms and disorders
- ❏ High blood pressure
- ❏ Gallbladder disorders
- ❏ Stroke
- ❏ Heart attack
- ❏ Digestive disorders

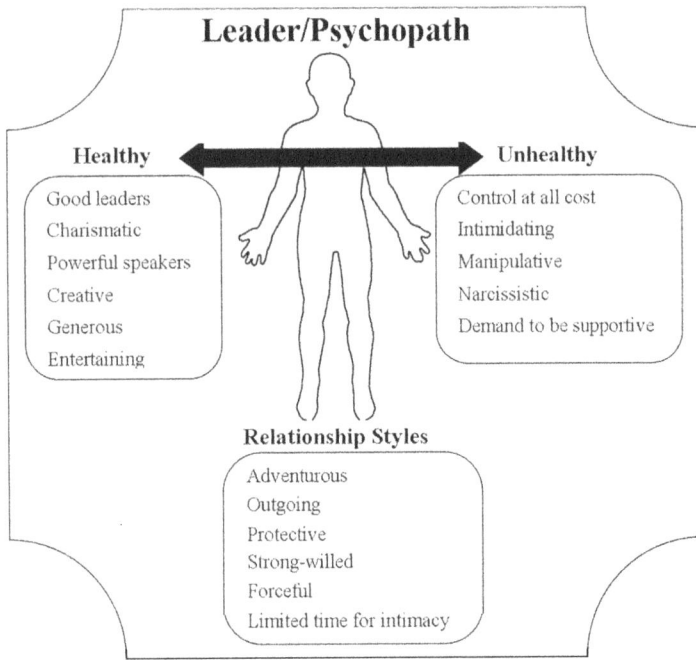

Leader/Psychopath

Healthy — Unhealthy

Healthy	Unhealthy
Good leaders	Control at all cost
Charismatic	Intimidating
Powerful speakers	Manipulative
Creative	Narcissistic
Generous	Demand to be supportive
Entertaining	

Relationship Styles

Adventurous
Outgoing
Protective
Strong-willed
Forceful
Limited time for intimacy

Achiever/Rigid

This is the last of the five personality types. I like to refer to this one as the Dynamo. The Achiver can become exceptionally proficient in anything structured. Because of their disciplined nature, they make great dancers, architects, designers, painters, or sculptors. They are good with music and languages, skilled with words and grammar. They are masters of order when it comes to maps, lists, systems, and analysis. They understand how things fit together, and can break down processes to design workflow systems. They have a high respect for laws, rules, and boundaries.

They are considered "left brain" linear thinkers, and are methodical when thinking and reasoning. They have a strong ability to focus in a clear and logical manner. They can prioritize well. Performing well is important to them, and they want to be as competitive as they can in anything they do. They are excellent at taking a project from start to finish and executing it skillfully.

The Rigid's body is typically well-formed and proportionate; they have bright eyes and good skin color. Their gestures are graceful, and they have a tendency to hold their head high and their back straight. They tend to have a very athletic look with good symmetry.

They commonly suffer from disorders of the heart, lungs, thymus, breasts, and arms as well as from asthma and immune system deficiencies.

Relationships

Rigids' tend to believe that their partner will see their trying to correct or improve them as acts of caring. This can be viewed as criticism by the other person, while the Rigid sees it as an act of love. Their expressions of love tend to be controlled and appropriate rather than passionate and spontaneous.

John and Nancy had met six months before on Match.com. They enjoyed dining out, and John always picked the best restaurants. Often, when they would be seated, John would make sure that Nancy immediately put her napkin on her lap, and frequently did it for her. This became a problem for Nancy, since, as she said to John, "I can put the napkin on my lap, thank you." In John's mind, he wanted to make sure Nancy's dress did not get any stains on it, because she always wore beautiful and expensive clothes. He viewed his actions as loving; she viewed them as intrusive.

Rigids' tend to be extremely attractive to women, partly because of their looks but mostly because of the energy they give off. A male may become a 'womanizer' to reinforce a sense of virility without the need to commit to love. They tend to marry more than once, as the intent is there to commit to one woman, but once in a committed relationship, they hold back and then search for love elsewhere.

The Rigid or their neglected partner may have an affair outside their relationship. They tend to seek out a "confidante" who can share in the emotional "heart to heart" without sex, and then have another partner to whom they submit sexually but withhold their heart. Sometimes their main relationship becomes more like brother and sister, though they maintain the facade to everyone as the "perfect couple."

In relationships, they are often judgmental when others don't meet their unrealistic standards. In their marriage or partnership, they will work hard to be the perfect partner. And if their partner is having problems, they will work hard to fix them so that they, too, are perfect. However, they can't fix anyone except themselves. If their partner doesn't change, they will be reluctant to end the relationship. It is important they not stay in a relationship just to keep up appearances or because they think they should be perfect enough to fix it.

Dynamos' have intense fears of having their "hearts broken" in love.

Popular Actors/Characters

Some familiar examples of this type of personality are Monica from *Friends*, Felix from *The Odd Couple*, the Tin Man from *The Wizard of Oz*, Will from *Will and Grace*, Hermione from *Harry Potter*, Mitt Romney, and Hillary Clinton.

Rigid/Perfectionist Checklist

Check off all that apply:

Healthy Behavior

❏ High Achiever

❏ Self-confident

❏ Organized

❏ Responsible

❏ Predictable

❏ Fastidious workers

Unhealthy Behavior

❏ Disconnected from emotions

❏ Over-achievers

❏ Must be right all the time

❏ Righteous superiority

Relationship Style

❏ Maintains healthy boundaries

❏ Capable of great love

❏ Open to growth

- Competitive
- Have all the right answers

Common Illnesses

- Heart disease
- Lungs
- Thymus
- Asthma
- Circulation
- Obsessive-compulsive disorder

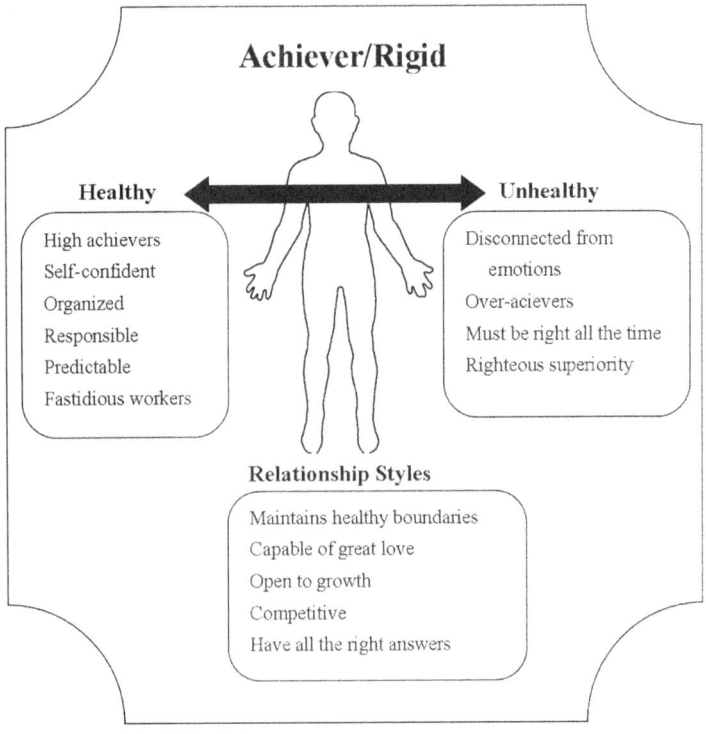

Character Structure Checklist

Check off two character structures in each category. This will give you a snapshot of the type of person that might be compatible with your personality. The four checkboxes consist of yourself, the type of men you've dated in past relationships, and the types of men you want to date or avoid.

	Me	Past Relationships	Men Desire	Avoid
Creative/Schizoid	☐	☐	☐	☐
Empathetic/Oral	☐	☐	☐	☐
Nurturer/Masochist	☐	☐	☐	☐
Leader/Psychopath	☐	☐	☐	☐
Achiever/Rigid	☐	☐	☐	☐

Chapter 5
BALANCE

Once you have gone through the assessment, you should have an understanding of what areas in your life and behavior you have chosen to balance. Balance requires clear thoughts without distractions. I will share some basic techniques on how to get out of the unhealthy patterns of each of the character structures. Since they are all different, the techniques may vary. Remember, it is within your power to shift into a healthy state of mind!

Whenever you become conscious of going into an unhealthy behavior pattern, the first thing to do is to get back to being present. Initially, it may appear to be counter-intuitive, as unhealthy behavior is actually a way of coping with whatever is happening at the moment. Why would you even consider taking away your coping mechanism? Your response to the pattern will most likely be defensive, which will most likely bring you a negative outcome. It is possible to break the auto-response by taking a moment to "step back" and evaluate before responding. This will allow you to "tap in" to your life experience and wisdom, that which you have spent a lifetime acquiring.

When I am having a bad day, I ask myself "what energy am I putting out there? That's what I'm attracting right back". It is also true that people who hold on to an unhealthy character behavior will react to my personality based on theirs. It's not anyone's fault, and once you understand the behavior patterns it makes a lot more sense as to how and why people interact to you the way they do. I do not take anything personally, and have learned how to assess others quickly and in a non-judgmental way. That's the beauty of all of it!

Each of these character structures contains a survival pattern that a person has developed in order to cope with the problems they face in everyday life. The strategy to find balance is to use the healing skills to break out of the pattern and back into being present and positive. Staying "present" is what gives you the skills to navigate through life and respond to the situation here and now in a way that will bring you success instead of staying caught in the past and doing something that was conditioned into your body back then. These skills will also help you understand other people's dynamics and decide how best to deal with them.

Getting Yourself out of Unhealthy Behavior Patterns

Creative/Schizoid

The unhealthy behavior of the Creative/Schizoid feels like you are completely ungrounded, and have lost a solid connection with your body. Your mind races and your thoughts are fragmented, and there is a feeling of wanting to "escape" from reality, for whatever the reason is. Sometimes it doesn't take much to feel this way, and the slightest event can trigger these feelings because you are not grounded.

Take a deep breath, plant your feet firmly on the ground, bend your knees and keep your eyes open. Now repeat the phrase "I will connect to the earth" slowly, and notice the frequency of your voice. Connect that frequency to your body, let your voice flow through it. Allow the energy from the ground to flow up your body, like you are a tree and your feet are the roots.

Empathetic/Oral

Unlike the Creative/Schizoid, the Empathetic/Oral feels drained from trying to be everything to everybody. The end result that is needed to shift is the same in all the character behaviors, and that is to get back to being present. It is important to realize that you don't need to give or get from anyone else, and work on giving to yourself first. Once you realize that the energy you have given away to others to nurture and support them is enough to support yourself, and whatever you then have available to others is what you can provide them without depleting your energy. It is not selfish to take care of yourself first; it's the only way to have the energy to help others. A good example is when the stewardess explains on a flight about the oxygen mask—put the mask on yourself first and then you will be able to help your children.

Nurturer/Masochist

The Nurturer/Masochist feels "heavy and stuck" like you just can't get anything done. You are used to practicing "self-sabotage" which keeps you stuck from moving ahead.

Move your body concentrating in the hip area. Stand up, walk or jump up and down. This movement will get your energy flowing. Thirty minutes of exercise a day will help you get "unstuck" and get out of a sluggish mindset.

Leader/Psychopath

The Leader/Psychopath's main focus is to release aggressive/ defensive behavior pattern. The breathing/grounding technique is helpful as explained in the Creative/Schizoid example above. Since there is usually very little hidden anger with this character structure, cultivating anger management techniques or simply slowing down and breathing, keeping your feet on the ground would be a good start. It's not uncommon to be your biggest critic also, so cut yourself a break! Remember that one of the best personality traits is being a leader, which is well within your power!

Achiever/Rigid

The Achiever is a perfectionist by nature. When things don't seem to be going as planned, anxiety, frustration and disappointment can rear its' ugly head. If you are trying hard to make the world more organized, your best strategy is to relax! You are the only one who is going to be hardest on yourself. So, the grounding/breathing technique is recommended. You can also shift your attention from perfection to playful. Picture a puppy in your mind, playing with a stick. The puppy sees nothing but the stick and gets great pleasure in chasing it. A simple concept! Life is too short to worry so much.

For all of the character structures, once you sense you're in the unhealthy behavior of a pattern, the first thing you should do is step back and become present again. There is a technique to re-center yourself that takes about five seconds:

1. Straighten your back (but don't stiffen it)

2. Inhale and let the breath move up your spine

3. Exhale deeply.

I always love seeing the positive changes in women once they get to this step, because they begin to manifest what they truly want out of life, not from fear, but from an authentic place. It helps to be present and let go of white noise so you can look through a clear filter at the world around you.

Chapter 6
CHANGE

How would your life be different if you stopped worry-
ing about things you can't control and started focusing
on the things you can? Let today be the day you free
yourself from unnecessary worry, Seize the day and
take effective action on things you can change."
- Steve Maraboli, *Life, the Truth, and Being Free*

There is no doubt that change is not easy for many people. Even when we know we need to make a change, it is often more comfortable to stay in a "safe" place which allows us to know what to expect, regardless of the outcome.

Lasting change requires preparation. Wouldn't it be nice if you could share your progress with friends and family, even small changes? This does not require it to be on New Years' day, as we all know most New Years' resolutions fail. The best time to start is now. Don't share that you are going to make changes either, because if you don't follow through you will feel like you've failed.

So what is required to actually make prepare to make changes? Here are a few key points to help gain the momentum to make positive changes:

1. Find the underlying reason why you want the change, not just because you "should". The reason needs to be strong enough for you to stick with it, and once you decide on what that change will be, stick to it! Learning decision-making skills is a necessary part of change success. As you learn to decide and follow through, you will find that it becomes easier to make decisions to change. Also, start with a small change first, allow yourself to fail until you get it right. But don't give up!

2. Give yourself some preparation time. This lead time will give you the space to learn how to cultivate your decision making skills. This timeframe may be a few hours or days, but don't take too long, because distractions will rear their ugly head. Also, don't wait until the last minute either. Use that time to train yourself to become decisive. Forty-eight hours might be a good place to start

3. Use your imagination! When you are wondering how to accomplish the change, imagine that you've already done it. Ask yourself how you did it. What you are actually doing is helping yourself "map out" how the change can be accomplished. This is an excellent technique to help overcome obstacles. Remember, you've designated lead time for this purpose.

4. Don't give up! Remember, it takes a lot of courage to make changes, and obstacles area natural part of the process. Resilience is built on trial and error, and only when you are able to pick yourself up and dust yourself off will you understand what it takes to get to the end result.

5. Celebrate your success, no matter how small! Take baby steps, try different decision techniques, and learn from each one you use. Once you have mastered a technique with a small change, you will become excited to move on to bigger ones. Eventually, you won't even need to strategize, it will come naturally.

We must all learn to live our lives in love rather than fear, and trust in our individuality, for only then will we be ready to lead an authentic life. We must learn to stand alone and think for ourselves without fear of how others judge us. This is so important in decision making for becoming a change agent. Make changes for yourself, based on your own needs.

So go ahead: Listen to your intuition, develop trust in yourself, and have the faith to think outside of the box. One small mindset change may bring you the man you have been searching for all your life, and wouldn't have seen if you were still looking through that cloudy filter. It certainly did for me.

In a coaching capacity, whenever I am working with a client who recognizes that changes need to be made, it is best to take baby steps so that it is never overwhelming, and the changes made will stick for the long haul. It is important to give yourself time, and it is not uncommon for it to take up to six months for changes to actually stick.

Where to Start

The best place to start is to identify what is within your power to change in your life and what is not. There are obvious distinctions between the two, and the reason you need to do this first is so you can set aside the areas that on which you are no longer going to waste your precious energy.

Things You Have No Control Over

Age. We are all aging, and the more you worry about getting older, the quicker you will age. If you spend 365 days worrying about getting old, a full year will have passed you by. You will be a year older, but you will have missed the whole thing instead of enjoying yourself.

Nature. Nothing is more out of our control than Mother Nature. We can attempt to plan a vacation, an outdoor party or a hike in the woods, but ultimately we have nothing to do with the outcome. It's even hard for a weatherman, even with the most scientific equipment!

Time. It seems the older I get the quicker time flies! The best we can do with time is to make the most of it. It becomes more precious when we don't have enough of it.

Other people. Although it appears that we sometimes have control over others, we really don't, only when they allow us to or they are our own children. Even then it's difficult if they have a mind of their own.

The past. We can't control the past, but we can control the future.

Things You Can Control

Diet. You have control over what you put into your mouth, and how much you eat.

Exercise. You have the choice to exercise or not, with the obvious limitations.

Date. You can choose not only if you want to date but also who you date.

Behavior. How you choose to behave is based on what you know at the time in your life. Your behavior can also influence how others behave toward you for the most part.

Knowing the difference between things you have control over and things you don't is the key to saving yourself a ton of time and frustration. Some things just won't be fixed by frustration. When you struggle with things you can't control, you prolong the nasty feelings that come along with it. You might get angry because you don't have control over it, or you might feel weak because you can't change it. You might even lash out at others. When you realize that it is not within your control, you have an opportunity to retake your power.

Chapter 7
DATING OVER 50

As I mentioned, my adult dating experiences started when I was 46 and newly divorced. I had spent my 20s in a career, got married at 30, had my first child at 36, and the second at 38. I spent the next 13 years as a stay-at-home mom raising my daughters. While my girls were still home but didn't need me as much, I began the next phase. I had no idea how I was going to meet someone new and had never enjoyed the idea of dating multiple people, as I was always a "one-man woman." I also lacked the confidence to feel I had something to bring to the table. I had always been a people pleaser and didn't know how to say no to anything.

Let's start with some basic relationship questions. How well do you communicate? Do you smile often? Are you approach-able? How confident are you when it comes to dating? Are you comfortable meeting someone on a blind date, or do you prefer speaking to them first?

Gaining the confidence to begin dating again is well within your power, you can have fun with being whoever you want to be, as no one will know you!

There are things you can do to look our best. Do you have a little black dress for any occasion? Is your lipstick the perfect shade for you? Is it time to treat yourself to a manicure or pedicure? What about your killer smile? Men love women who smile!

These skills are essential, but their power is limited. If this is your only strategy, you're missing a big chunk of the puzzle that could make or break your success!

It's important to get a clear picture about where you stand on a few things so you know what you're looking for:

♦ Your beliefs about men

♦ Your ideas about relationships

♦ Your beliefs about good available men

♦ Your past relationship history

♦ Your relationship intentions

When you qualify where you stand, you are able to create a dating scenario that suits you. That's the objective for developing a brilliant diamond mindset!

Have you ever wondered how that average-looking woman landed the perfect guy? Chances are she knew what she wanted and took the time to learn how to get what she wanted by tapping into what was her genuine beauty and positive spirit. She released the negativity that was holding her back from finding what was there waiting for her. How much time are you going to spend wondering how to get to the other side? Well, it's time to make a new and exciting plan for you!

Dating isn't always easy, and the challenges women sometimes face can be discouraging. It's important for you to identify what those challenges have been for you so that you can fine-tune your objectives for change. Since we have all lived for more than half a century, there isn't much we haven't experienced in any or all of those areas, in our love life, careers, family or health. So let's take a look at some common challenges.

"I've given up Looking."

If you reach your 50s and things haven't worked out the way you planned, it's not unusual to give up looking. We have learned through the years to be independent in our careers, take care of ourselves and others, and often put ourselves last. We have opportunities now that former generations never had, including the choice to stay single. But if your choice in a mate has not worked out in your favor, it may be time to reevaluate the expectations you have set for yourself. So many women set themselves up for failure because they have unrealistic expectations of meeting someone new. It doesn't help when women feel the signs of age, and when they look in the mirror, they feel old. Men experience the same thing. In a perfect world, everyone would like to meet someone good-looking, fit, healthy, and prosperous. But that may not be realistic.

Unfortunately, many women come out of a divorce with very little to show financially, because they either stayed home and didn't work or were not the breadwinner with the 401K. That makes it difficult later on when they go back into the dating world feeling like they have nothing to offer.

Here are a few reasons women give up on looking:

- ◆ "I want to protect myself from getting hurt."
- ◆ "What will my kids think?"
- ◆ "What if I get rejected?"
- ◆ "I'm too old to be dating."
- ◆ "I'm too set in my ways."
- ◆ "I can't find anyone in my town, I don't want to travel for more than five miles, and it's too much effort."
- ◆ "If we don't have the same background (kids, career, etc.), it probably won't work."

♦ "I don't want to bother with someone that has any health issues; I'm not going to be a caregiver."

♦ "I have no interest in exercising."

♦ "I have no interest in sex, and I don't want to take my clothes off."

♦ "I'm tired and don't want to put any effort into anything."

♦ "I'm better off alone; I'm unlovable."

♦ "It's hard to find someone to trust so that I won't bother."

Instead of thinking of 100 reasons why you don't want to meet someone new, why not think of just one reason why you would? What would your reason be? Try thinking small, like meeting for a cup of coffee or dinner. No pressure, just a good time with someone new. Start with a clean slate—no expectations, no judgment.

Alone or Lonely?

Loneliness is designed to help you discover who you are, and to stop looking outside yourself for your worth."

– Unknown

How many times have you woken up in the middle of the night feeling completely alone? The silence, which is usually peaceful, appears to put a stranglehold on your heart. One evening as I was awake, I put my thoughts on hold and just embraced the quiet that surrounded me. What I realized was that this silence was a beautiful thing, and I took the time to close my eyes and breathe. I decided to turn my fear of silence and loneliness into an early morning sanctuary all curled up under the covers. How wonderful to have a peaceful and warm place to lay my head down at night. "I am blessed," I told myself.

You can be just as lonely in a crowded room filled with friends. I guess it depends on what filter you're looking through. Loneliness is a response to isolation or a lack of companionship. Sometimes all someone needs is a cat or a dog, and they are happy. It's just as nice for the animal, as they also have the need for companionship.

The first thing you want to do is find out the reasons why you feel lonely. Is there a particular time of the day, week, or year? Does boredom play a part in your loneliness? Social media has made it worse. People have disconnected from regular conversations with others, and our attention span has gotten shorter. Always checking for text messages and social media posts has turned us into tech junkies; we now measure our self-importance against the number of "likes" we get for that photo of the muffin we ate for breakfast. Have you ever tried to have a conversation with someone only to be interrupted by them taking a phone call in the middle of your conversation, or constantly checking text messages while you're talking? Most people don't even realize they are doing it; it's become part of our culture. Not only is it rude, but it's also just not healthy.

One thing that may help better define your loneliness would be to write in a journal when you're feeling lonely. Writing down your current thoughts can help you release them, and you may find that it clears your head—you can always find what you were thinking on paper. I used to write poetry. Most of it was dark and depressing, but it gave me a creative outlet.

Loneliness is a part of being human, and you are not alone. I can't knock social media altogether, as Facebook can be an excellent venue for those who are isolated or alone. It seems to be getting more popular with the over-70 age group, too, as they become a bit more computer savvy with either laptops or IPads. Now you can be anywhere and connect with friends and loved ones.

Learning to enjoy your alone time can make all the difference in the world. Being alone provides you with the quiet time to clear your thoughts and decide how you want to use it. As I always say, "If you can stand your own company when you're alone, you can do anything!"

There are some fantastic online learning portals that provide opportunities to get involved in different college or certification courses. With online learning, not only can you spend your free time learning something new, but the online friends you meet in the classes have the same interest as you. Who knows, you may even meet someone in the class who may want to get to know you!

Fears

Our minds are powerful. Fear is something that can easily overtake our subconscious mind and cause havoc. Unfortunately, when fear takes over, there isn't much anyone can say to alleviate it. Whether it is fear for your safety or fear of abandonment, it is debilitating. For the sake of what is relevant in this book, let's discuss the most common relationship worries.

Fear of Abandonment

This is the most common concern. If you fear abandonment, you most likely think that people who love you will leave you, or even die. One has to wonder how a person's death has anything to do with someone else feeling abandoned, but it does. Even if you feel someone is not there for you, abandonment is the critical issue.

This fear is so deep for most of us that we don't even realize we feel it. Most people don't sit there and make the connection. If you were in an environment as an infant or young child where you felt unsafe, were abused, or didn't have anyone close to you that you could trust, you naturally will feel abandoned, and that feeling becomes ingrained in your psyche for your whole life. It's not easy to recognize and then release without help from a professional counselor or life coach.

"I'm Not Good Enough."

This is a common fear about not being perfect. Rejection is a theme that resonates with those who feel they have to live up to some illusion of perfection or get rejected. It's hard to look around and not feel like a failure if you listen to those around you who have high expectations or are looking for the perfect person. Well, guess what: perfection doesn't exist! If we all realized this when we were younger, this point would not even come up.

"I'm a Failure."

Similar to "I'm not good enough," some people feel that failure is inevitable. But let's think about this for a minute. How do you define failure? It's a broad term that may hold true for something like a school test, but is hard to gauge in life. Our failures in life become our most prized possessions; if it weren't for any failures, we wouldn't get ahead in life. I'm proud of my failures, as they have defined my incredibly resilient personality.

I could write a book just about fears, but in the end, we all can identify them within ourselves. The most valuable part about that is, once we identify them we can work on alleviating the cause, which we will cover in future chapters in this book.

"I'm Not Perfect."

So many women over 50 feel they need to live up to the expectations of a model. "I'm too fat" and "I'm too old" are two of the most common fears. I'm not going to spend too much time on these except to break it to you in the most uncomplicated way—guys just don't care about your weight or your age. If you are ten pounds overweight and have a bit of a roll, no one cares but you. There are no perfect men, and if there were, they wouldn't be able to find the ideal woman at the perfect weight. Your fears are getting in the way of your happiness. So stop worrying and start living. There is no better advice I can give you than that.

Temporary Setbacks

Women are pretty resilient by nature, but having temporary setbacks can be a recipe for possible depression and exhaustion. Failures can be demoralizing if the world knows about them. We don't bounce back as quickly, which can make them all the more painful. If you feel like you have no control over the outcome, you are likely to feel hopeless, and fear will set in, making it worse. It's important to find ways to regain control of whatever it was that happened so you can avoid feeling helpless. Here are some examples:

You keep trying new diets and fail every time. You begin to beat yourself up once again, blaming your lack of willpower. Instead of blaming yourself, you might want to rethink what diets you are trying, as eating styles are a personal choice and not all diets work for everyone. You've been on a dating website for some time, and you are not getting any responses. You feel unattractive and boring. Since the profile you present is the first thing people read, you decide to rework it and make yourself more marketable, so you have a friend review and make comments. Typical sentences like, "I'm looking for someone trustworthy and friendly" just don't cut it. Beef up your profile and see how that works. Also, have someone take a nice picture when you are looking your best.

You get an interview for a job and you are one of two candidates, you have a 50/50 chance of getting the job. You think you did pretty well on the interview, but not only do you not get the job, they never call you, so you're sitting and waiting until you finally realize you're not getting a call either way. As disappointing as it may seem at the time, most likely it wasn't a good fit, and you weren't meant to be there. Setbacks are never easy, and we don't have any choice except to keep moving forward. Just don't look back. Trust me; there is always a reason why things happen the way they do. It's just not always that obvious.

Deal Breakers

Usually, deal breakers in any relationship are not negotiable. Some common deal breakers include money issues, substance abuse, not wanting to have children, or political differences.

It's helpful to review your list and see if there is anything on it that can be eliminated. Here are some examples:

- ♦ No smokers
- ♦ No mimics
- ♦ No road ragers
- ♦ No rude guys
- ♦ No gawkers (respect the woman you're with)
- ♦ Lack of personal hygiene

So go ahead and make your list. I would love to hear from you to see what's on it!

Relationship Basics

Dating in our 50s is not something most of us ever imagined we would be doing when we were in our 20s or 30s. We couldn't even imagine being in our 50s; it seemed so old. Back then, we had the time to screw things up, as time wasn't even on our radar screen. Fast forward 30 years: Are you still looking for the same things in a man that you were back then? My goodness, I hope not! You've grown up, acquired life skills, and have a bucket filled with valuable life lessons that can withstand the test of time. You have grown as a woman. But it can also be true that the filter you view life through has become quite cloudy as your accumulated baggage began to pile up.

Expectations

Do you have higher expectations than you did when you were 20? Conversely, has your reality become so marred that you have resigned yourself to becoming whoever the person that dates you would like you to be?

If you've been fortunate enough to have a decent selection of prospective dates, you probably have set your expectations high already, and the list gets longer as you keep dating. It gets exhausting! Here are some of the most common dating expectations:

Example 1: "I want an epic love story. I want all the passion, drama, and everything in between, so I have an incredible story to tell my grandchildren." Realistically, you want to build something healthy. Love isn't something that's found; it's created. You don't need to have the pain to have passion.

Example 2: "A relationship will make me happy. There's just something missing from my life. I don't feel whole or complete; I'm bored and just don't quite feel fulfilled. Finding someone to love and who loves me back will fix that." Realistically, relationships are for you to share; happiness comes from within yourself. Being happy on your own gives you the ability to make healthy decisions for yourself. You choose to be with someone else because you want to, not because you have to. When you rely on someone else to fulfill your needs, this will lead to an unhealthy level of dependency and resentment.

Example 3: "You and I are always 'we'. We go everywhere together; I can't exist without you." Realistically, that's a lot of pressure to put on your partner. Maybe he would like time to do things he likes without you. This expectation runs the risk of collapsing. Keeping your individuality is important for both yourself and your partner.

Example 4: "Things will never go wrong; we've got a set of rules to follow that can't be violated." Realistically, that's not possible to maintain, nor should it be. There needs to be room for error, flexibility, and compromise. Things go wrong in life, and it's unrealistic to think your relationship is above some high threshold. Perfection doesn't exist.

Different Types of Relationships

Once we reach our 50s and beyond, there are two good reasons to have a relationship—love or companionship, or both. If you are lucky, you will have both! There are other types of relationships that should be avoided if you are looking for a partner for life. One is a "relationship of convenience" where one person puts themselves ahead of the other and just wants to get together when it's convenient and otherwise have separate social lives. Another is when your one person tries to dominate the other. You will continually be draining your precious energy on this type of relationship.

If you are dating a "rebounder," it's likely the guy can't be alone for a minute, and you certainly will be a welcome addition to his space—you or anyone who is available. Are people in their 50s interested in open relationships? If you're into being in a committed relationship but don't mind sharing other partners, go for it. This may be suitable for some, and is an option if you choose to take that road.

The Reasons Why Relationships Fail

If you are in your 50s and have been in a relationship, you have experienced the feeling of failure when things don't work out. Feeling the loss of a relationship is not the road anyone wants to travel down, but understanding the lessons of that failure will hopefully bring you success the next time around. No one ever goes into a long-term relationship hoping it craps out, and sometimes you don't see the end coming. It could suddenly rear its ugly head without warning.

Here are some common reasons why relationships fail:

1. Trust Issues—We all go into a relationship with the hope that trust will always be there. When trust becomes an issue, it's like poison to a couple. If the relationship is worth salvaging, there is always the option of counseling, in the hopes that, with guidance, trust can be regained.

2. Different Expectations—Two people are drawn together by similar expectations in areas like physical attraction, sexual compatibility, common interests, family values, and similar socio-economic backgrounds. If the expectations are not the same or change during the time the couple is together, it could present problems.

3. Moving through Life at Different Speeds—When one partner is growing at a fast pace while the other is stagnant, there may be some conflicts that arise. Change does not come easy to some, and so the change that is occurring for one partner may cause discontent to the other. Sometimes couples become less compatible as they get older due to personal growth changes.

4. Communication Issues—Lack of communication is a general reason for relationship breakups, as anger and disrespect work their way into daily life. Sometimes when we are in emotional pain, it's common for us to either lash out in anger or clam

up. There is also the chance that intentions could be misinterpreted due to lack of communication.

5. Relational Abuse—Any form of emotional or physical abuse in a relationship is a reason for a relationship to fail. This also includes one partner dominating and trying to control the other.

6. Addictions—Gambling, drugs, and alcohol are just a few everyday habits that hurt and sometimes destroy a relationship.

7. Boredom—It's not uncommon for couples who have been together for some time to experience boredom, or the feeling that they are in a rut. It's important to have common interests to share that help keep the relationship interesting. The daily grind of child-rearing, a job, school, or house maintenance sometimes gets in the way of being mutually involved with each other. One example is when the grown children leave home and the parents experience "empty nest" syndrome. They suddenly feel like strangers to one another, as they have not focused on each other for some time.

8. Financial Issues—If one person is a saver and the other a spender, there is a good chance there will be some money matters that get in the way. A couple also doesn't need to be married to have money challenges.

There Is Someone for Everyone

Patty had been dating on and off for a few years after her marriage fell apart and she got divorced. She lived in the same town where she was busy raising her twins, who were now in middle school. After attending many school events, she struck up a friendship with another local man who had a son in the same grade as Patty's twins. Ron had also been recently divorced and was interested in dating again. Ron and Patty spent time together as friends, but Ron was more interested in taking the relationship to the next level.

Patty wasn't much interested in more, as she was looking for someone taller and a bit younger. After about six months of casual dating, Ron was over fixing a leaking faucet in Patty's house. All at once, what she once considered a "non-contender" became someone she saw as the perfect man for her. What was it about Patty's mindset that changed at that moment in time?

What Patty finally realized was the man who was "perfect" for her was not what she envisioned in her list of conditions. Because there were no distractions and her filter was clear, she was able to see that this man was more compatible with her than she would have ever imagined. Now, for those who are expecting Mr. Right to come in a perfectly tailored package with a big bright bow, know that you will never receive him. He doesn't exist. Just as you are not perfect, a man looking for the perfect woman will never find her. But a man looking for a beautiful woman who can give love and accept him for who he is does exist. You need to realize that you are perfect just as you are, and so are the men searching for someone like you.

So you want to "have it all"... what is your "all"? Let's be realistic for a moment. Your "all" is quite different now than it was when you were 20, and if it's not, it should be. You've lived in this world long enough to have stories to tell and experiences to share, and if you're not tired of difficult relationships, you should be. There should be a point where you seek simplicity because that is a very attainable goal.

Depending on what kind of man you want in your life, there are two choices—a good one or a bad one. The defining factor is: how does the man make you feel, good or bad? It doesn't get simpler than that. The better you feel about yourself, the stronger your choice will be to choose a good man. By this time you should want nothing less, which is why you are reading this book.

Now you may want a good man, but are you a good woman? Good men want the same thing, no exception. Are you defensive, demanding, negative, or critical? If you answer yes to any of these, you need to take a closer look at why you have any or all of those behavior patterns.

What Are Good Men Looking for in Women over 50?

Frank is a happily married man in a marriage for over 35 years. I asked him what he would be looking for in a woman if he was suddenly single. His response: "Have you noticed the single men on a Friday night pasted against the bar walls scared to death to talk to the women around them? I would be frightened out of my skin to approach any single woman, as they are all unapproachable. I wouldn't have the slightest idea how to approach any one of them."

Pete is an average guy working in construction. He comes into the local bar every night for a happy hour beer before he goes home. Pete has been happily single for many years, creeping up on 50 years old. When I asked him what he is looking for in a woman, he had one statement: "I don't want a woman to try to change me. I like to play golf with my buddies and come to happy hour for one beer after. I just want someone who gets me." Men are simple thinkers for the most part. Don't you want the same, a man "who gets me"?

Men are pragmatic by nature. When faced with a problem, they tend to come up with more simplistic solutions without complications. This is where the differences lie. While most women would be thinking the man is not listening, he may not be if there is too much "white noise." Men don't understand drama, so it's not surprising that they would tune you out with too much detail. There are some men who have more of an emotional personality, and those types of men would engage in conversation about whatever emotional drama is being discussed.

Fine-tune Your "Creep Meter"

Every time Susan goes out, she is approached by what she considers "creeps." These men all seem to be suffocating and controlling, and always seem to want to tell her what to do. She doesn't know why it happens to her all the time, and she gets frustrated because no one who approaches her is even halfway decent.

What Susan fails to realize is that she is subconsciously sending some negative energy out; she may feel "negative" attention is better than no attention. This is a typical unhealthy behavior pattern of the oral character, and she is actually attracting exactly who she's asking for. Energetically, what you give out is what you get back. You don't have to be a creep to get a creep, but if you are continually being approached by the wrong men, you need to do some "self" work.

How does Susan stop the pattern and change the type of attention she is receiving? Once you have mastered the art of positive energy, you may slowly begin to see a shift in the types of encounters you have with men. In fact, the number of interactions with jerks will decrease considerably, and if you do have one you can chalk it up to the jerk not having any filter at all! Creeps are everywhere, and you can't help how they act. You can, however, take control of how you respond.

Manipulators

Sandy has been dating a man she met on Match.com for about two months. Every time they go out to dinner, he guides her to the meal of his choice, not hers. She reluctantly complies, constantly feeling manipulated, but never says anything.

Manipulating behavior is a common behavior pattern of the Leader/Psychopath character structure, and if this man is already exhibiting signs of manipulation, chances are it will only get worse. Manipulating men are good at pulling your strings, and even the smartest, most well-balanced women can fall for these types of men.

All women should want a good man in their life, one who is compatible, loving, and kind. Good men want the same thing, so your goal should be to become just that. At the very least, fine-tune what you already have to offer.

Sensuality

There is nothing more appealing to a man than a sensual woman. Sensuality is a very personal thing. Some women have never experienced it or do not see themselves as sensual or sexual at all, especially as we get older. When you start to "feel old" you think your sensuality disappears. Here's the bottom line: Men don't age as well as women, so our odds go up. We have greater sensual capacity well into our later years, as it becomes a state of mind. The more you feel or believe in being sensual, the more it happens to become real. Sensuality is how in tune you are with your senses. Do you notice smells, textures, sounds?

There is a benefit to being older, and that is the wisdom that comes with the package. You can't compare the knowledge (or lack of) between a thirty-something and a fifty-something, it's one of the life's gifts. Don't ever discount the value it brings to a relationship.

When I was in my 20s, the thought of dating in my 50s never entered into my mind. One reason was I thought that most people got married and stayed married, or if they lost their spouse, they would most likely not date again. As time went on, and women became more independent, working for a living, it became more common for families to separate and each to take on a new life with different partners. My life changed too.

For those of you who are back in the dating world for the first time, things have changed dramatically. With technology evolving at the speed of light, where it was once common to pick up the phone and call someone, we now have texting, Facebook, and online dating. It can be overwhelming if you have not been exposed to it until now.

Most of us have evolved to some degree with technology, especially if we are still in the workforce. My work experience has been quite advanced technologically all along, so I'm pretty savvy when it comes to weeding through all the junk. I thought it would be worthwhile to discuss a few key areas in regard to online dating sites and dating safety.

Places Men Go

I went grocery shopping on Valentine's Day evening around 6:00. As I walked around the store filling up my grocery cart, I noticed many men carrying flowers and stopping in to pick up a card for their significant other. I also noticed men without flowers picking up their steaks and beer. I remember thinking, "If I were single, I'd be shopping at the store on Valentine's Day evening, because it was obvious that many of these guys are single!" I have a friend who works at Whole Foods, and she tells me all the time about all the single guys she knows who pick up prepared meals after work. That sounds like a good place, because they are also eating healthy!

There are many places where single men go on a daily basis, and if you are out and about, you may see them. Just check out your local gas station around 7:30 in the morning!

Restaurant bars are another good place to go. Men tend to be comfortable sitting at a bar alone eating a meal. Next time you spot one, head over to order a drink and ask him how his meal is.

The local hardware store or Home Depot is another good place to check out. I spend a lot of time there, since as a homeowner I'm always buying stuff, and there is never a shortage of men walking around shopping. It's easy to strike up a conversation about anything in the store, and most men would be happy to share their knowledge with you.

Meetup.com is another place to meet men. Join one in your community, maybe a business networking or over-50 group. At the least you'll meet people with the same interests as you.

ONLINE DATING

When it comes to online dating, it can be quite overwhelming with all the dating sites out there. Back in 2003, I was a stay-at-home mom raising two young daughters when I ended up getting divorced. Luckily my ex is nice, and we always kept a friendly relationship, not only for the sake of our girls but because it was an option we both chose. For most women, that option is not available because one or the other has decided to relate negatively or angrily. I'm not passing judgment on who treats who like dirt, just saying that we were lucky to have the better option.

Once I got divorced, it was difficult for me to believe I had something to offer anyone. I was not working, I was living in a family-oriented community west of Hartford … who would be interested in a divorced mother of two with no job? Back then, online dating was relatively new, and a lot less complicated than it is now. My suggestion is that if you haven't been on before, you may want to sign up for free just to check it out, and not post a picture right away, maybe even hide your profile until you decide, that way you can check it out beforehand. Now let's talk about the most popular ones.

Match.com

Match.com is the most popular for all ages, and was one of the originals. I got on Match.com back in 2003, and the format is the same. It's pretty straightforward, but probably not the best site for over-50 dating, as some of the others are geared more toward that age group. Writing a winning profile is important. We'll cover that later in the chapter.

eHarmony.com

eHarmony is geared more to finding a compatible person who has the same personal qualities, like kindness and loyalty. They will ask you to rate yourself in a bunch of areas, including feelings, skills, relationship beliefs, and other personal areas. Based on your answers, they will send you matches each day. The cost is between $12 and $40 per month, depending on the length of time. You can't view matches unless you sign up.

OurTime.com

This site is pretty straightforward. You can create a profile for free and search for compatible dates. You can view profiles safely without disclosing who you are. This seems to be a decent online dating site for seniors.

POF.com (Plentyoffish.com)

This is a free online dating site. I know a few people who have met good men here. One met her future husband. They've been happily married for a few years.

SeniorPeopleMeet.com

Similar to OurTime.com

Online dating—2017 Statistics

There are a lot of online dating statistics available. Let's start out by looking at some of the more interesting ones. There were three primary reasons the participants used online dating: to find a long term relationship, to find someone to have a good time with, and to easily pre-screen dates. They also found it easier to have conversations online with strangers.

In April 2017, a survey revealed the following stats:

♦ 84% of dating users were looking for a romantic relationship

♦ 43% used online dating for "just friends" contact

♦ 24% used online dating apps for sexual encounters

♦ Match.com was the most popular online dating site (3.44 million paid subscribers in the US alone with a monthly revenue of $1.3 million)

♦ Total number of single people in the US: 54,350,000

♦ Total number of people in the US who have tried online dating: 49,650,000

♦ Total eHarmony members: 17,500,000

♦ Total Match.com members: 24,575,000

♦ Annual revenue from the online dating industry: $1,935,000,000

♦ Average spent by dating site customer per year: $243

♦ Percentage of male online dating users: 52.4%

♦ Percentage of female online dating users: 47.6%

♦ Percent of breakups in online relationships that happen by email: 48%

Sources: statisticbrain.com and statista.com

Writing an Online Dating Profile

The profile you create on an online dating site is the first introduction a man has to you. You are marketing yourself to the male population online. What we say about ourselves is no different than what we present to the male population we want to get to know. We show our best side. Your profile should show you off in a way that will catch a man's eye. Since this is your first impression, you want your profile to sound flirty and fun. Here are a few pointers on what to focus on:

1. Be approachable. You want a man to feel like you would be willing to meet him without fear of rejection. An open, kind, and honest profile is a good place to start. List your best qualities and be confident. You will be a man magnet when you feel good about yourself.

2. Be grammatically correct. Nothing is worse than bad spelling and messy sentences. It shows you didn't put much time and effort into it.

3. Don't lie about your age. You don't want to start out in any relationship with a lie, especially if you also say you are looking for someone honest and trustworthy. Part of the self-empowerment lesson here is to embrace your age and be accepting of the fact that everyone is aging at the same speed, including the men you are looking to connect with. You wouldn't want someone to lie to you, so don't do it to them.

4. Don't be demanding. First impressions matter, and unless you are looking for a man who will be a doormat, don't start the conversation with demands.

5. Be authentic. There is nothing better than being who you say you are when you meet someone. The more authentically you present yourself, the less energy it will take to live up to what you described, and you will be more likely to attract someone who is more compatible.

6. End with a statement that will catch a man's eye, and get him to think, "I have to contact this woman, I have nothing to lose."

The Online World

If you have been out of the dating scene for some time, the reality is that the world has changed. What was once a connected society of telephone conversations and group gatherings has now become a virtual community. If you have joined the ranks of women who embrace this new world, it is equally important and necessary to be diligent about your safety without being fearful. The balance then becomes combining the digital tools with the personal interactions.

It would be a perfect world if all of us could easily integrate the two without getting frightened or frustrated, and I can tell you it is possible! My 83-year-old mother is now on Facebook, downloading family pictures to print and put in her photo album. So it is possible to move along "at the speed of your internet service" in whatever way works for you.

Safe Online Dating—Tips Every Women Should Know

With all new dating apps or online dating options to meet new people, there are more safety concerns than ever before. While meeting and making quick connections through online dating is easy, a lot of risks are involved. With so many news stories about Internet dating scams, identity theft, financial fraud, Internet stalking and catfishing, the fear among online daters is justified.

Here are some useful tips that will help you to avoid trouble and have an enjoyable online dating experience:

1. Choose your online dating site wisely. If you haven't used any dating site previously, then you might want to take the time to review which ones might be the best for the over-50 crowd. Always use reputable sites that protect your information and ask for your permission before sharing your information with others. A legitimate site will protect your information, but most likely will not verify the users' background.

2. Make sure you don't have too much personal information in your dating profile and that have the ability to make your profile "private" when necessary. Never disclose where you work or live.

3. Do not share your phone number on the first chat, wait until you feel comfortable.

4. Concentrate on the conversation. It's not easy to find "red flags," so take your time until you feel you can trust that person. Trust your instincts!

5. Red flag questions include too much personal information too soon, or if the conversation sounds too good to be true.

6. Always report inappropriate behavior to the online dating site. You'll be saving someone else the headaches of having to deal with this person, and it's just the right thing to do. After you report him, block him.

7. Always make sure to do a quick background check, which can reveal criminal records, financial records, real names, and addresses. It's a good idea to be one step ahead of him. You can start with doing your free research, which I will map out later in this chapter.

8. Never meet a man at his home or your home until you have finished a right background check. The exception will be if you meet someone through a friend.

9. Always make sure to share all details with a reliable friend or family member who can be around in case of emergency.

10. Have your friend text you during the date to find out if things are going well. Create a "secret alert" word to text if you need help.

11. Always have an exit plan in case the date is not going well, and you feel you need to get out early.

12. Always drive yourself in your vehicle. You don't want to be on someone else's dating schedule. Otherwise, the other person will have control of how long the date is and when he will drop you off.

13. Don't drink alcohol on the first date. You want your instincts to be on target.

It is always better to be safe than sorry. Remember, if things go well it will lead to a second date and beyond!

Background Checks

It is a good idea to use a background check service while dating unless the person you're dating was recommended by a good friend or family member. There are several ways to get a background check done. The least expensive way is to do it yourself with some online tools; the second is to use an online background check service; and the third is to hire a private investigator, which can provide more extensive and "real-time" information.

♦ Free Background Checks. The first place you'd start is to do a Google search on a name in quotes. "John Smith" obviously will come up with hundreds of thousands of hits, so the more you know, the better your search will be. The second place to check is a site called peekyou.com. PeekYou looks for links that are associated with the person you seek online. When it finds the information, it indexes all the links in one place for easy browsing. You will get an overview, and you can also search by categories such as interests, work, city, phone, and email. It's pretty scary as to how much information is available to the public for free. Try doing a search on yourself. Next, you can search by an image. If you have a dating profile picture, you can copy/ paste it, go to Google, and do an image search. It will look for similar images from websites such as LinkedIn or Facebook. Next, you can search the sex offenders' website (www.nsopw.gov). It allows for many different searches, including cities and states.

♦ Online Background Check Services. There are many websites that offer background checks for a small fee, including sites like Spokeo, BeenVerified, and TruthFinder. These websites just may give you the information you are looking for. The downside is that if the data is not updated regularly, you will never know if you are getting the latest and greatest.

♦ Private Investigator. If you have had a bad experience with online background checking services, or you think your date may be into something unlawful or severe, this would be your next option. I guess I would say that if you feel you need to investigate a date with this option you may not want to be dating him at all!

What's Your "No"?

I grew up as a people pleaser and rarely said no to anything. I didn't understand the value of my own time, and also didn't want to disappoint anyone. I drew most of my self-worth from thinking, "If only I say yes, I will be of value to the other person." This is not healthy, and the more you say yes to things you either have no time to do or should not be doing, the less value it has for anyone. Many women have a problem saying no, whether it is in regard to making a commitment for their time, a ride to the store, or a friend borrowing money.

So how do you say no? Here are some examples from *The Oxford Dictionary*: nope, no way, out of the question, negative, no siree, not on your life, not for all the tea in China, under no circumstances—well, you get the picture! Personally, none of those work for me. I have found using the statement, "I think I'll pass, but thank you" works.

Now, although all of the words and phrases listed above say no, some women still may not feel comfortable using any of them as their way of refusing. Why does it matter? Has there ever been a time in your life when you said yes to someone when your gut told you no? Were you taught at a young age to be polite and never say no? For whatever reason, saying no is important, as it creates a necessary boundary in which other people will respect your time.

Many women were taught at an early age that saying "yes" was polite. It became part of our daily ritual, and a core belief that being nice meant saying yes. Fast forward, and it's clear that if "yes" is a big part of your vocabulary, you have a need to be a people pleaser and saying yes makes you feel of value. You might also believe that the more you say yes to, the more important you are. Otherwise, why would people ask you for something unless you were needed?

I know it is hard to say no sometimes because we never want to let people down, and we'd rather deal with our negative feelings than deal with the guilt that people might place upon us for declining.

So the question remains, is there a way to say "no" without feeling guilty? Absolutely!

Feeling guilty for saying "no" is an indication that we do not have any idea how to prioritize our time. If you had your priorities straight, you would naturally process the request in your "calendar database" to see if there were any other commitments that you had going on. Using a calendar program on your phone is one of the best ways to keep your schedule straight. It's right at your fingertips.

Sometimes saying yes just adds to the distractions in your daily life. Something's on the calendar you know you have to take care of, but you would rather go out for happy hour, so you say yes. All that ends up doing is making the time that you have to get the thing done that you put off a lot shorter, and that can be very frustrating. So, saying yes can sometimes lead to frustration. So how can you say no nicely? Take a moment before giving the answer, as you need to weigh what's against it. Here's one way to say no: "Thank you so much for thinking of me. Unfortunately, I will have to pass, but I appreciate it."

Practice saying "no" with kindness. You will not only gain the respect of the party requesting your help, but will also gain respect for yourself because you value your own time.

Intuition

Intuition is something you should trust. It's your body's way of sending you a signal because it's picking up something. I have learned to trust mine, and I always say that I would rather be wrong than not listen to it. So, if you're out on a date and your gut is screaming, pay attention!

Chapter 8
LEARNING TO LOVE AGAIN

Trust

If you are a woman over 50 and you are reading this book, the chance that you have made it to this point in your life without some trauma or life-changing event is unlikely. Our past experiences, whether marriage, sexual or emotional abuse, the death of a loved one, an unexpected accident, or a health challenge, set the stage for our daily thoughts and beliefs.

Trust (or lack of trust) is one area that does not just change overnight; it takes a lot of support and self-reflection to get to the point where your beliefs shift. Ideally, you want to get to the point where you can forgive and "not forget," but the "not forget" must only be the life lesson learned, and not the wound.

Even if you take ownership of a failed marriage by acknowledging that you may have contributed to its demise, it does you no good to have regrets about past behavior as in "if only I had…." Newsflash: You did the best you could with what you knew at the time.

Fears

Whenever you experience fear, no matter what it is, the thoughts you carry can wreak havoc on your body. Stress and anxiety affect your physical and mental well-being. What happens to your body energetically? Here are some examples of what happens when you become fearful or acknowledge a negative thought:

1. You lose your job and don't have much money saved. The job market isn't that great, and your house payment is due. You may have to tap into your limited 401k until you get another job. All of a sudden you begin to experience a leaky bladder, and one night you wet the bed.

2. You are dating a nice guy but are not completely sure if he is "the one." You have established a commitment already, but are thinking that you don't want to go any further if he is not "the one." Things are going smoothly, so there is no reason to break up. You begin to experience pressure in the eyes, and your eyesight becomes a bit blurry. You keep a set of cheater glasses nearby in case your eyesight isn't clear.

The next time you experience a health challenge, no matter how small, especially if it doesn't make any sense, stop and think about what is going on in your life at the moment. Your body provides a roadmap for you to follow; you just need to be aware of it.

Get More Enjoyment out of Your Relationships

To improve your relationship dynamics with others, you need to be willing to "go deeper." This requires a willingness to go beneath the surface and experience more of what's going on in your life. Examine things that will help you have better relationships. This requires going deeper within yourself first. Taking the time to understand your flawed thought process will show your prospective partner that you have an interest in improving your view on relationships and will set a good example and encourage him to do the same, to work together to become stronger. Going deeper will teach you to be aware of the stories we tell ourselves that keep us down and disempowered. You will recognize when you're going into "story mode," and align with more positive beliefs that serve you. Ask yourself what's going on beneath the surface that is affecting what filter you look through.

When you focus on the positive, good things happen. You begin to express yourself more positively, and, because of that, you have a greater chance to be heard. You will not put the other person in a defensive mode, as you know it is next to impossible to communicate if you or the other person is defensive.

You also need to set up personal boundaries, not during or after you have issues, but right at the beginning. Limits are necessary to create a safe place where you can create freedom and have defined rules to follow. If you set up a few rules, it will be easier to keep them.

I've been dating the same man for over 14 years. When we first met, I remember having an emotional conversation with him (I don't recall what the subject was), pouring my heart out. I looked at him, and he was staring at the ceiling. When I asked him what he was looking at he said, "There's a fly on the ceiling." He had completely tuned me out!

It's important to understand that men are biologically different than women, so it's not uncommon for men to disengage from complex emotional discussions. They are just not wired the same.

Developing communication techniques that get you the result you are looking for is a necessary goal for any couple. You will learn the different communication styles in my program, which is based on the different personality character structures I've already told you about that define each of us. By the way, the communication techniques will help you in your job, talking to your kids, or any other situation once you understand the differences in personalities.

No matter what culture, age, or language, there are five communication styles that people use: blaming, placating, being reasonable, distracting, and being congruent. When you blame someone, you take away the value of the other person. When you placate, you bring value to the other person but diminish it within yourself. When you are "super reasonable," you disconnect from your feelings. First, you go into your head; you tell yourself, "I know it's supposed to be this way," but you are not connected to your emotions. You can be right in your mind, but you won't connect with people. People around you will think you are looking down at them. When you are distracted, you make a joke or change the subject. You are not communicating, and the other person gets frustrated and doesn't feel like you're listening. When you are congruent, you are paying attention to both your own needs and those of the other person.

Although each of these communication styles has a place in conversation as long as you are supportive of the other person, it works best when both parties are congruent. Then they both have each other's best interests in mind and work together to solve the problem.

Think of a family situation in which mom and dad are arguing, mom is blaming dad, dad is placating, and the child is distracting both parents by running around the house. Distracting mom and dad isn't a bad thing; in fact, the child instinctively knows that it may work to bring mom and dad together again!

It's helpful to be willing to give up your position in a dis-agreement. That doesn't make you weak or wrong, but it allows the other person to have value. It ties into a congruent commu-nication style. If someone says "I'm right," and you feel you are right, you could say something like, "You could be right, and I could be wrong. Let's discuss it and find out the truth." It's a great way to negotiate!

Another way is to "go with the flow," or taking a step closer to them, which can bring the relationship closer together. It shows you value them, and that they are being heard. For example, let's say Mary is upset that John didn't take out the garbage. "You didn't take the trash out as I told you to. And you never remembered to bring in the newspaper when you got home from work," she says. John's responds, "Gee; I'm so sorry, I'll take it out now." John doesn't have to agree with Mary, but his response says that he's connected with Mary, hears her, and values her more than he needs to be right.

Chapter 9
A HEALTHIER YOU!

All the dates in the world can happen, but if you are not feeling your best, you won't be your best. Having a healthy mindset includes feeling good physically.

There are many health challenges that women over 50 can experience, and I could write a book just on that! But I want to concentrate specifically on hormone health in this book, as many hormonal imbalance symptoms can improve through diet and lifestyle changes. Also, the use of high-quality essential oils can play a significant role in positive health changes when used along with diet and lifestyle.

As a coach, I am not authorized to diagnose or recommend anything in particular, if you are experiencing a problem, it is necessary to consult the proper medical doctor, preferably an endocrinologist who specializes in hormone conditions. My job is to support you at the place you are at with a correct diagnosis. Then, the recommendations in this book can be considered to incorporate into your wellness routine. Also, not all foods or essential oils may interest you, and the information provided is an overall summary of what has been known to work historically for those who have the same symptoms as described in the book.

So let's get right into the endocrine system, which plays a huge role in the hormone system in your body. We know that your endocrine system secretes hormones, and regulates many bodily processes such as your metabolism, your stress response, your sexual function, sugar metabolism, mineral homeostasis, heart rate, digestion, reproduction, sleep, and mood. Also, it affects almost every cell and organ and tissue in your body. The organs that make up your endocrine system include your pituitary gland, thyroid gland, parathyroid gland, adrenal gland, pancreas, and ovaries.

Essential Oils and Hormone Health

Let's talk about some of the best essential oils to use and how essential oils help. There's a study on rose essential oil in which they found it inhibited stress-induced symptoms in lab rats and naturally increased certain stress hormones and reduced the elevation of neuronal activity. We know cortisone is frequently referenced as the aging hormone. So if you get too much cortisone, cholesterol stays too high, human growth hormone remains too low, it can cause aging or premature aging symptoms as well.

Let's talk about some common conditions related to the endocrine system.

Adrenal Fatigue

When your brain registers a threat, the body releases adrenaline hormones to help you react (known as the "fight-or-flight" response). The adrenal cortex then releases corticosteroids to inhibit processes such as digestion, immune system response and other functions not necessary for immediate survival. Adrenal fatigue occurs when the body and adrenal glands can't keep up with the amount of daily stress many people experience, and those "unnecessary functions" become neglected for extended periods of time.

Most people struggle with adrenal fatigue at some point in their lives. Common symptoms include weight gain, insomnia, reduced sex drive, body aches, trouble concentrating, racing thoughts, irritability, feeling tired, hormone imbalance and food cravings.

More people are struggling with adrenal fatigue than ever before. Typically its' cause is when somebody is overdoing it, working too much and not resting enough—you've heard the term "burning two ends of the candle." If that happens, it will burn out the adrenal glands. An example would be if a lion were chasing you, you're either going to fight it, or you're going to run from it. Either way, your body is sending all of its nutrients and all of its energy, to its extremities; when this happens cortisone levels rise. So when that happens over time, your adrenals secrete and are responsible for adrenalin and cortisol for those hormones.

So with adrenal fatigue, what happens today is most of the time we don't have a bear or a mountain lion chasing us, but we live in this high state of fight or flight all the time. It's stressful at work and money or family situations. We don't take a day or two off on the weekends. We're bringing kids to soccer and basketball practice. We are so busy we can't stop and breathe. Moms have it worse than most. For women over 50, it may be a constant fear of getting sick or running out of money, or if they have a fear of losing a job at the age of 56 or 60.

Imagine your adrenal glands are pumping out hormones. They're pumping out cortisol. They're working with adrenalin. All these are happening. Finally, they say, "I'm burnt out. I'm tired. I can't keep it up anymore." That is adrenal fatigue. So if you're a person who goes to bed at night, and even after getting a good night's sleep, you're still tired the next day or frazzled, that's adrenal fatigue.

One of the most beneficial essentials oils is holy basil, this is one of the herbs used as part of Ayurvedic medicine in India.

There is a term called adaptogens or adaptogenic herbs. These are herbs that help lower cortisone, which helps your body better adapt and deal with stress. So, the most powerful and potent essential oil for balancing hormones and acting as an adaptogen is holy basil essential oil. And the benefits of holy basil are tremendous! It's the one I recommend for women struggling with adrenal fatigue or chronic hormone imbalance of any kind, including the thyroid or adrenal issues.

The next beneficial essential oil is rosemary oil. This oil is used for issues with blood sugar, inflammation, for supporting hormones like DHT and supporting the brain. These two in combination, if I were recommending just two oils, would be my top two oils. Now there's also a compound in clove oil called eugenol, which is also found in holy basil, that acts as an anti-oxidant, as well as a natural adaptogen. And then rose oil, as well, which naturally improves mood, and supports energy levels.

As far as supplementation for adrenal fatigue, the top two I would recommend would be ashwagandha and a Vitamin B-complex. Ashwagandha and B-complex help support the adrenals. Also, eating a clean diet, which includes bone broth, along with a lot of dark-colored nutrient-dense fruits and vegetables that are black or blue. Blueberries, seaweed, and black rice would be in that category.

Depression

Depression is a common mood disorder caused by changes in brain chemistry. It affects approximately 14.8 million American adults. Symptoms include fatigue, sadness, low sex drive, lack of appetite, feelings of helplessness and disinterest in regular activities. Research indicates that other factors contribute to the onset of depression, including genetics, changes in hormone levels, grief or difficult life circumstances. Antidepressant medications have side effects that can include suicidal thoughts, weight gain, and personality changes.

Depression is something so many people struggle with, and it's shocking the number of people that are diagnosed with clinical depression. In fact, some of the top prescribed medications today are anti-depressant or anti-anxiety medications. The dangerous thing about anti-depressant medications is the side effects. They can cause suicidal thoughts. They can cause lack of motivation. They can cause other chronic illnesses with vitamin and mineral deficiencies in the body. The good news is essential oils work with the body in an all-natural way.

Some of the best essential oils used for depression include bergamot oil, as well as other oils like orange or neroli oil, ylang-ylang, lavender, and chamomile. Lavender and Roman chamomile are great for reducing any emotional stress-related symptoms and naturally improve the mood. For supplements, I would recommend fish oil and Vitamin D3. For seasonal depression, a high-quality fish oil or Omega-3 supplement with Vitamin D3 would be helpful. Dr. Josh Axe recommends 5,000 IUs twice a day, especially in winter months.

Hypothyroidism

Hypothyroidism is a condition related to having an underactive thyroid gland that doesn't make or release thyroid hormones. The thyroid gland releases hormones that move throughout the bloodstream and reach receptors that are found throughout the body, so a disturbance in thyroid function can cause noticeable health problems. According to some estimates, 40 percent of the population suffers from low thyroid function. Common symptoms of hypothyroidism include a slow metabolism, poor digestion, low energy levels, increased carbohydrate cravings, trouble sleeping, depression, thinning hair and signs of accelerated aging.

Holy basil is one of the best essential oils to use. It acts as an adaptogen in lowering stress and balancing out cortisol levels. To use this oil, rub directly on the thyroid area. In small doses, some of these can be used internally in capsule form or as a supplement. Myrrh oil is also useful as it helps get rid of dampness. It's great for the digestive system and mood. Lemongrass oil is beneficial, especially if someone has Hashimoto's thyroiditis, and chamomile oil, as well. Chamomile oil helps reduce emotional stress. So these oils in combination, probably the most beneficial for the thyroid, with holy basil being number one for sure.

From a supplement standpoint, ashwagandha is the king of the herbs when it comes to benefitting the thyroid. So for thyroid health, ashwagandha and holy basil, that combo, is going to be the most powerful. There are clinical studies on ashwagandha as a supplement showing it helps balance out TSH levels, T3 levels, T4 levels, all of the thyroid hormones and markers.

Also, if somebody has regular hypothyroidism without the autoimmune form, iodine should be considered. Now, and you may go to a doctor or endocrinologist and get iodine levels tested. If somebody has Hashimoto's thyroiditis, they want to be careful or probably not take iodine because often, the issue is the body's not absorbing iodine. It can cause a goiter if they're doing a lot of iodine with Hashimoto's Disease, and adding selenium would help. I would say if somebody has any form of hypothyroidism, I would recommend ashwagandha, selenium, as well as a B-complex vitamin. They might also, rather than taking iodine, just do some green superfoods where they're getting a little bit of iodine from seaweed such as kelp, spirulina, chlorella, that type of thing, but that's what I would recommend for the thyroid.

If somebody has the autoimmune form of hypothyroidism, a lot of those health problems begin in the gut with leaky gut syndrome. So when you have leaky gut syndrome, there are holes in your gut to where certain foods or proteins can leak through the gut wall, then get into the bloodstream, causing inflammation throughout the body. So if somebody has hypothyroidism, often the connection is a digestive issue.

As mentioned with adrenal fatigue earlier, the cause could be emotional stress plus diet. Hypothyroidism is related to diet and also related to the digestive lining. A diet including foods like bone broth, soups, lots of things that are very easy to digest, or going grain-free with hypothyroidism, except for maybe some rice. I would do some slow-cooked rice, lots of fruits and vegetables, things that are easy to digest and focus on a diet that's also going to help heal the gut lining as well. A diet rich in collagen can be beneficial.

Menopause

Menopause is the natural decline in reproductive hormones that begins when a woman reaches her 40s or 50s. The duration is very hard to predict, as each woman's situation is vastly different. Women typically begin experiencing hot flashes, mood swings, vaginal dryness and other menopausal symptoms during peri-menopause. This stage is considered part of the menopause period and can last from 10 months to four years, as the ovaries gradually decrease estrogen production. However, menopause is not considered to have officially begun until a woman misses her period for 12 consecutive months. Menopause is the natural biological process; although it ends fertility, women can stay healthy and vital.

The most effective essential oil for menopause is clary sage. Clary sage is beneficial because of its ability to balance out estrogen levels in the body and raise them during that menopause time. Another is roman chamomile, really great for reducing stress, mainly because it supports the nervous system. Peppermint oil has a very cooling effect on the body as well. It can help reduce that excess heat.

One of the most prominent side effects that many women deal with during menopause is hot flashes. Doing peppermint oil on the bottom of the feet and within the body is excellent as well. And thyme oil thyme is helpful because as sage, it has been shown to help with progesterone balance, but also it helps with circulation in the body. So, thyme, clary sage, chamomile, and peppermint, a great blend to do. Lavender can also benefit the body.

Some herbs within Chinese medicine like black cohosh is one of the best herbs, probably the most prescribed herbs for women who are going through menopause. Wild yam extract is often used in this way as well. Also, doing a vitamin B-complex can have great benefits as well for those struggling with menopause symptoms.

Premenstrual Syndrome (PMS)

Premenstrual syndrome (PMS) is another condition worth mentioning, although it usually affects a younger age group. PMS symptoms are linked to the menstrual cycle. These symptoms include mood swings, bloating, acne, tender breasts, food cravings, irritability, fatigue, headache, and depression. Changes in hormones during the menstruation seem to be a common cause; chemical changes in the brain may be a factor. Emotional stress does not seem to cause PMS, but they may make it worse. About 3 to 8 percent of women have a more severe form of PMS, called premenstrual dysphoric disorder (PMDD), which can be debilitating. The good news is that if you improve your diet, manage stress and implement natural remedies, you can experience significant improvements in the symptoms associated with PMS.

A few of the most beneficial essential oils for PMS are holy basil and clary sage. They can balance cortisol as well as estrogen. Now, cypress oil is useful because of its ability to improve circulation. That's one of the things you want to do during PMS. You want to support your body in blood circulation throughout the body as well. Cypress can help with that also. You can do a few drops rubbing it on the lower abdominal area is where you want to use that. You can also use ylang-ylang oil, that helps with improving your mood. Clary sage has more sedating effects, holy basil has more energizing effects, and ylang-ylang helps with the more positive outlook and energizing the body as well. One of the best supplements for PMS would be a Vitamin B-complex supplement.

Weight Gain/Obesity

"Overweight" and "obesity" are both labels for ranges of weight that are greater than what is considered healthy for a certain height. An adult who has a BMI between 25 and 29.9 is deemed to be overweight. An adult who has a BMI of 30 or higher is considered obese. Excess weight is often caused by an overconsumption of calories and physical inactivity. Other causes may include stress, hormonal imbalances, medical conditions, genetics, toxins or certain medications. The good news is there are steps to address weight gain and obesity naturally, which include eating a healthy diet, following a healthy lifestyle (including regular exercise three or more times per week) and using natural supplements.

If somebody is struggling to lose weight, here are some of the most effective essential oils. Cinnamon oil helps balance something in the body called glucose tolerance factor (GTF). This oil is also beneficial for diabetes and blood sugar, but cinnamon, great for blood sugar, which can reduce sugar cravings and help support weight loss. Grapefruit oil contains compounds that may reduce cravings for certain sweets. Ginger oil is very warming and aids in digestion. It has anti-inflammatory benefits that can help the body. Black pepper oil has also been known to promote thermogenesis because it's very warming in the body. It has been shown to potentially reduce addictive behavior.

There are a few diets that are beneficial. I think doing a keto-genic diet, along with intermittent fasting are beneficial or doing both together. A ketogenic diet may be a good choice for these type of health conditions. As with all diets, check with your doctor first. Often, if you do ketogenic longer than a year, it can start to create some deficiencies in the body, but a ketogenic diet, which is cutting carbs, eating a diet that's higher fat and protein, almost no carbs at all. The ketogenic diet is the diet recommended by Dr. Josh Axe. You can do a lot of meat and a lot of vegetables, in an intermittent fashion where you just drink bone broth for breakfast, and you only eat your meals at noon, mid-afternoon (3:00 pm) and early evening (6:00 pm). That's the fastest way I've seen for people to lose weight is combine ketogenic and intermittent fasting for a period of time. Long-term, I believe the key to having a healthy weight is focusing on getting three things in your meals, protein, or especially protein and fiber. Now healthy fasting is another thing to do when you're following ketogenic, but in general, protein and fiber. A protein made from bone broth powder or bone broth is the protein recom-mended consuming every day. Lots of fiber from fruits, vegetables, seeds like flax seeds every single day, and then probiotics.

If you want to lose weight, remember diet's first, exercise second. Essential oils can be used third in combination as part of a program to help support weight loss as well, and help fight obesity.

Effective Oils

Bergamot: Can create feelings of joy and energy by boosting circulation of the blood.[1]

Black Pepper: Naturally warms the body and may stimulate the metabolism.[2]

Chamomile: Improves thyroid health while helping to reduce the effects of stress and to promote restful sleep.

Cinnamon: Contains the compound cinnamaldehyde, which promotes healthy blood sugar balance.

Clary Sage: Helps to balance hormones naturally.

Clove: A powerful inflammation-cooling agent that can boost energy.

Cypress: Improves circulation and relieves cramps and aches.

Ginger: Helps to cool excess systemic inflammation and improve digestion.

Grapefruit: May reduce cravings for sweets and boost metabolism.

Holy Basil: Helps to soothe anxiety. This is shown to regulate serum cortisol levels, which can impact immune system function, memory, learning ability, mood, and weight. Works as an adaptogen to naturally balance cortisol levels, promote a healthy response to stress and encourage healthy thyroid hormones.[3]

Lavender: Lavender is known to address neurological issues positively, it can also be used to help with insomnia and headaches Rose: Shown to promote calm, relaxation and to balance blood pressure.

Lemongrass: Soothes inflammation and balances insulin, which supports thyroid health.[4]

Myrrh: May relieve red, dry and flaking skin by cooling inflammation.

Peppermint: Helps cool the body during hot flashes; has a hormone-balancing effect.

Roman Chamomile: Inhaling may help lessen anxiety and general poor mood or mental outlook.

Rosemary: Helps to balance cortisol levels; boosts mood and supports a healthy memory.

Thyme: May delay menopause by stimulating hormones; helps relieve menopausal symptoms, including mood swings, hot flashes and insomnia.[5]

Ylang-Ylang: Acts as a mild sedative and can lower stress responses, such as an increased heartbeat and high blood pressure.

1   Hongratanaworakit, T. (2011, August). Aroma-therapeutic effects of massage blended with essential oils on humans. Nat Prod Commun. Retrieved from www.ncbi.nlm.nih.gov/pubmed/21922934

2   (2011). Health Benefits of Black Pepper Essential Oil. Organic Facts. Retrieved from www.organicfacts.net/health-benefits/essential-oils/health-benefits-of-black-pepper-essential-oil.html

3   Gholap, S., Kar, A. (2004). Hypoglycaemic effects of some plant extracts are possibly mediated through inhibition in corticosteroid concentration. Pharmazie; 59(11):876-878. Retrieved from www.ingentaconnect.com/contentone/govi/pharmaz/2004/00000059/00000011/art00014

4   Shah, G., Shri, R., Panchal, V., Sharma, N., Singh, B., Mann, A.S. (2011, March). The Scientific basis for the therapeutic use of Lemongrass. J Adv Pharm Technol Res. Retrieved from www.ncbi.nlm.nih.gov/pmc/articles/PMC3217679/

5   Zava, D.T., Dollbaum, C.M., Blen, M. (1998, March). Estrogen and progestin bioactivity of foods, herbs, and spices. *Proc Soc Exp Biol Med*. Retrieved from http://www.ncbi.nlm.nih.gov/pubmed/9492350

DIY Recipes

Adrenal Rejuvenating Blend

In a roll-on glass bottle, combine 15 drops jojoba oil, 15 drops holy basil oil, two (2) drops rosemary oil and two (2) drops peppermint oil. Roll the mixture onto your back, just above the kidneys, up to three times daily.

Invigorating Inhalation

Rub one (1) drop each of bergamot, lavender and ylang-ylang oils into the hands and cup the mouth and nose. Breathe in the oil slowly. Also, try rubbing the oils on the feet and stomach.

Warm Adrenal Compress

Dilute 3 to 5 drops of holy basil or rosemary essential oil in a carrier oil and apply it directly to the skin over the kidney area. Next, add a warm compress. The oil mixture can also be applied to the reflex points on the feet.

Thyroid Support

Rub 2 to 4 drops each of lemongrass oil and myrrh oil directly on the thyroid area along with reflexology points on the feet (big toes) on the wrists multiple times per day.

Weight Management Boost

Add 1 to 3 drops of grapefruit oil to a glass of water three times daily, or add a blend of cinnamon, grapefruit, ginger and black pepper to a diffuser and take in deep breaths for two minutes, one to three times daily.

Hormone Balance Serum

Add 2 tablespoons evening primrose oil, 30 drops clary sage essential oil, 30 drops thyme essential oil and 30 drops ylang-ylang essential oil in a small glass bottle. Pour into a glass vial with a dropper. Rub 5 drops onto your neck twice daily.

For additional essential oil recipes, please visit www.draxe.com/natural-remedies-category/diy-recipes/

Suggested Supplements

Protein Powder Made from Bone Broth: High in easy-to-digest protein, this supplement may help support healthy blood sugar and metabolism.

Probiotics: Studies have shown improved weight management with probiotic use; it also helps to clear excess yeast, which may contribute to food cravings.

Ashwagandha: Ashwagandha helps hypothyroidism patients significantly increase thyroxine hormone levels, which can reduce the severity of the disorder.42

Iodine + Selenium: These supplements promote healthy thyroid function. If you have an autoimmune disease such as Hashimoto's, consult with a doctor before taking iodine.

Fish Oil: This is high in EPA, which is critical for healthy neurotransmitter function—an essential component in emotional and physiological brain balance.

Vitamin D3: This supplement helps boost vitamin D levels in the body, which can support a healthy mood and outlook.

Ashwagandha: An adaptogen, ashwagandha is especially good at balancing cortisol levels and helping the adrenals adjust to stress.

B-Complex: Vitamin B12 and other B vitamins soothe stress and improve cellular energy.

Chapter 10
THE BEST POSSIBLE YOU!

There is no doubt in my mind that there is someone for everyone on this planet. Now I can't guarantee that I will find your true love for you, since you are accountable for what you think and what you do. I can assure you that if and when you are ready to improve your outlook about yourself and others by following the steps I have outlined to understand your current mindset, you will be able to a) be the best you can be, and b) identify positive and negative behavior patterns in others. With an open mind and positive support, you will have the tools you need to move forward with enthusiasm and embrace what is waiting for you!

This process for change does not happen overnight. It will progress at the speed you feel comfortable with. For some of my clients, it was like a surge of energy all at once, and there was no stopping them! Remember, you have nowhere to go but up, and the choices you make to change are all for the better!

The biggest benefit of "being present" is the ability to manifest success in the world around you. Once you can look in the mirror and love what you see "as is," you are ready to explore the possibility of finding someone who will be compatible and live up to the realistic expectations of what you have set for yourself. You have value, first to yourself and then to others. It is not easy to ditch the judgment; it has to become a way of life to stop passing judgment on yourself and others.

Successful Love Begins at Home

There are many ways to be successful in love. Here's a list of my favorites:

Practice Forgiveness

When you forgive someone, you feel good. Each time you forgive, it gets easier and easier, until it becomes part of who you are.

Mirror Love

We all have both positive traits and the polar opposite "excessive" traits in our personalities. For instance, you may be a wonderful, nurturing volunteer for a nonprofit and then, at times, you are a needy manipulator. This is one example of the personality behavior of the Oral character structure, and at any given time you may behave either way. Those are two personality traits of the same person. To have success in love, you must search out someone who positively mirrors you. This does not mean that someone has to be exactly like you, but it does mean they should have positive traits similar to yourself. I am a very protective person, so the person who suits me has that same protective nature in them. I would not want a partner who I would always need to protect because the partner would then feel manipulatively needy. Does that make sense to you? People who have similar positive traits have a lot in common and enjoy doing similar things together. There is a saying, "When your kids leave home, you better like each other."

Be Kind to Others

Take every opportunity you can to say or do something nice for someone, every day. Do random acts of kindness for strangers and don't tell anyone what you did! If you make this part of your everyday life, you will find a large amount of kindness will come back to you.

Love Yourself First

Loving yourself is not selfish; it's required to have a happy and healthy life! Anyone who tells you otherwise is just wrong. You have to ask yourself, what filter is that person looking through? Do they love themselves? Most likely the answer would be that they don't.

We have been taught since childhood that it is selfish to put yourself first or to fulfill your needs first. What a lie! If that were the case, the advice from an airline pilot to "put the oxygen mask on yourself first so you can take care of your children" would be wrong.

Self-care goes beyond diet, skin care, and exercise. Self-care also means learning how to say no, speaking up when you need to, and telling your family that you need to be left alone for a bit just to have some quiet time.

You should create a space in your house or apartment that is your peaceful place or sanctuary. Mine is my living room. I am drawn to sit in silence looking out the window when things get hectic, I know I always have a place to escape and re-energize.

Things to Make You Go "WOW"!

There are so many excellent services for women over 50 that will get you into a perfect place. I've listed a few ideas here:

Photography Session

When was the last time you took the time to have some glamor shots taken? A few years back when I turned 58, I had the opportunity to do a photography shoot called Boudoir Belle by an incredible photographer, Paulette Mertes. I spent an afternoon dressing up and flirting with the camera! When I sat with Paulette and she showed me her favorite photos, I was shocked and said, "That's not me!" They were beautiful! To this day, I still can't believe I looked so beautiful!

What does a photo session like that entail? Take yourself shopping and buy a few things that you usually wouldn't buy for yourself. A pair of high heels, a soft shirt, anything that makes you feel sexy! Go to a department store where they offer image consultant services and tell them what you plan on doing. Trust the experts to pick out a few nice things for you, and just enjoy the attention you are giving yourself. The plan is to capture it in photos. Get your hair and makeup professionally done and enjoy the experience!

Image Consultant/Fashion Stylist

Image Consultants help clients improve their appearance for personal or professional reasons. They will help you to look and feel your best, gain confidence, and develop a style that is uniquely a reflection of you. Services offered range from personal shopping to a complete clothing makeover (learning to mix and match pieces). Some services also include hair and makeup. This is the icing on the cake, the finishing touch to creating the beautiful new you!

Massage

How wonderful it feels to get pampered on a table by a massage therapist! We should all make regular appointments, just like we do the oil change in our car.

Manicure/Pedicure

Doesn't it feel and look great when we spend the time to have our nails done! That's another thing we should regularly do.

Facial

Getting a facial is not only good for the skin, but it's also good for your health. Your skin is the biggest toxic eliminator, so getting regular facials is a "skin detox." It feels and looks fabulous!

Wouldn't it be an excellent idea to take a few of your favorite girlfriends and book a day at a spa? How awesome to spend a day pampering yourself, and having your best friends with you doing the same. Make it a twice a year event!

CONCLUSION

Don't spend too much time analyzing and criticizing yourself; you will just end up complicating your thoughts. It is necessary to let the less important stuff go, like what time the mailman delivered the mail, and wake up every morning with gratitude in your heart.

I hope you have found the information in this book helpful for you to be able to understand yourself better. It is the foundation you can build on to continue to give yourself the knowledge that you can use every day. If you are open to change, you will find there is no limit to the amount of information you will find to continue to make positive changes within yourself.

Even though energy medicine has been in my life since 1998, I learned even more about myself from writing this book. I am different than I was even five years ago, and if I read this book five years from now, I will learn something new about myself. That is because we are constantly evolving.

Throughout life, our body and mind are either in a state of regeneration or degeneration, with age as the one defining factor. For our mind, the improvement occurs when we fill it with positive thoughts and images, and our bodies when we fill them with healthy food. You are the only one who has complete control over your mind, which will ultimately influence your behavior and how the world sees you.

Have you ever noticed that when you wake up "on the wrong side of the bed," you end up having a crappy day? That, my friend, is the energy you send out to the world. I decided long ago that I was never going to have another bad day, no matter what happened. Was I always successful? No. Did that matter? No. It was the fact that I had made a conscious choice always to try. That has made all the difference in the world.

In closing, my advice to you is to do the same. You may find that your choice of a "happy filter" will be the start of a world filled with possibilities and options, most of which you never thought you had before.

FAQ'S ABOUT COACHING

What is a certified coach?

A certified coach offers guidance and inspiration to help clients shift their behavior to get more positive results in their relationships and health challenges. The best results happen when small changes are incorporated every week. Since every client has different needs, the changes that are recommended are a collaboration of ideas and individual needs between the client and the relationship coach.

Do I need to go an office to work with a coach?

No, most coaching sessions are not in person, but by telephone or video phone (e.g., Skype).

How often do I need to have a session?

Sessions are held once a week, and usually run about one hour.

If the coaching sessions involve health challenges, should I tell my doctor about working with a coach?

Absolutely! Most doctors would encourage you to take the initiative to make healthy lifestyle changes.

Do I have to share my medical history with a health coach?

Health coaches fall under the same privacy laws that other medical professional do. You only need to share what you think would benefit you.

What if there is something I want to talk about but am afraid of what the health coach will think?

Health coaches are trained to give their clients a "safe space." It is considered a "judgment-free" zone.

How long should I expect to work with a health coach?

Most unhealthy habits didn't happen overnight, and it's been found to have the most beneficial changes over a period of six months, which is the recommended timeframe. That is the average amount of time it's been proven to incorporate changes that stick.

I'm overweight and I've tried many different diets and nothing has worked. Can a relationship coach recommend a diet?

As a graduate of the Institute of Integrative Nutrition, I studied over 120 popular diet theories, and also work with clients to find the best weight management plan that fits their lifestyle. Everyone is different, and one person's diet style will be another person's poison.

REFERENCES

Eastern Body, Western Mind, Anodea Judith, 2004, Celestial Arts, USA.

Character Analysis, Wilhelm Reich, 1975, 5th enlarged edition, New York, Farrar, Straus and Giroux.

Bioenergetics, Alexander Lowen, 1976, Penguin Books, New York.

Language of the Body, Alexander Lowen, 1971, MacMillan, New York.

Character Styles, Stephen Johnson, 1994, W.W Norton & Co New York.

Characterological Transformation—The Hard Work Miracle, Stephen Johnson, 1985, W.W. Norton & Co New York.

Free Yourself 1—Releasing Your Unconscious Defense Patterns, Annie Marquier, 2005, Findhorn Press, Scotland.

Free Yourself 2—The Power of the Soul, Annie Marquier, 2005, Findhorn Press, Scotland.

Biology of Belief, Bruce Lipton, 2005, Mountain of Love/Elite Books, USA.

Core Energetics, John Pierrakos, 1990, LifeRhythm Publication.

Wilhelm Reich: The Evolution of His Work, Boadella David, 1973, Vision Press, Chicago.

Hands of Light: A Guide to Healing through the Human Energy Field, Barbara Brennan, Bantam, 1987

Your Body Sings Your Soul Dances, Dorothy Martin-Neville, PH.D., Garret Printing, 2008

Enjoy the Hell Out of Your Relationship, Ramone Yaciuk

Essential Oils and Hormone Health, The Essential Oil Institute, Dr. Josh Axe

Ogden, C.L., Carroll, M.D., Kit, B.K., Flegal, K.M. (2012). How many people are affected by/at risk for obesity and overweight? *Centers for Disease Control and Prevention.* Retrieved from https://www.nichd.nih.gov/health/topics/obesity/conditioninfo/Pages/risk.aspx

ACKNOWLEDGMENTS

I would like to thank Dr. Dorothy Martin Neville for her teachings at the Institute of Healing Arts & Sciences (IHAS). It was her teaching of the W.I.S.E™ method that brought me to an incredible level of awareness in energy medicine.

I want to thank my friends Andrea, Johnny, Steve, Honora, and those that requested to remain anonymous for their heartwarming and inspiring stories. It's your honesty and thoughtful contributions that have given depth and meaning to the message.

I want to thank Morgan Templar, a fellow author who took the time to voluntarily edit my book from a valuable perspective of a potential client. Her thoughtfulness and attention to detail is appreciated!

I want to thank all of the coaches and authors I have recently met through my classes and networking group. I have surrounded myself with like-minded, authentic pioneers whose journeys have brought us all together with one common thread—to share what we've learned to make a difference in people's lives.

To the Morgan James Publishing team: Special thanks to David Hancock, CEO & Founder for believing in me and my message. To my Author Relations Manager, Nia Baskfield, thanks for making the process seamless and easy. Many more thanks to everyone else, but especially Jim Howard, Bethany Marshall, and Nickcole Watkins.

ABOUT THE AUTHOR

Linda Yalen has experienced many of the same relationship challenges most women face. Her choices were never based on her own desires but on her belief of being a "people pleaser", tolerating verbal and physical abuse, a bi-product of low self-esteem. It was only after an assault and 19 years in an emotional crisis that she finally found a way to heal.

Linda has mastered the art of letting go of baggage and seeing things with clarity, learning from past mistakes and moving forward with a renewed sense of authenticity and positive energy. She helps others see the connection between the body's energy flow and beliefs and behaviors, heightening awareness of how a shift to a positive mindset can bring success in both health and relationships.

She also found relief with essential oils and diet changes that supported her ability to manage her menopausal symptoms, and studied the benefits of essential oils in order to help support women with their hormone imbalance challenges.

She joined the John Casablanca Modeling Agency in 2012 at the age of 57. "Age is just a number, and as long as I'm breathing I will continue to grow and change. Age brings you the courage to try new things, to share life's wisdom and to redefine the world around you."

Among her accomplishments:

- ♦ 2009—Energy Medicine Certification, Institute of Healing Arts and Sciences
- ♦ 2015—Certified Coach—Institute of Integrative Nutrition
- ♦ 2016—Anti-Inflammatory Nutrition Certification—Dr. Barry Sears, Ph.D.
- ♦ 2017—Essential Oils Coach—The Essential Oils Institute—Dr. Josh Axe

Linda coaches women using her Diamond Mindset program designed to bring awareness to what might be holding you back from relationship success. She brings a unique perspective to her clients by combining her energy medicine and relationship coaching to help women over 50 lead happier and healthier lives. She shares her positive energy to enrich those around her by bringing out the best in each one of her clients.

If you are ready to make changes in your life, simplify your thoughts and hold yourself accountable for your decisions, Linda will help you overcome any obstacle you may have. Her ability to share problem solving skills in relationships will allow you to lead a life filled with exactly what you deserve. Her goal for you is to be "eye catching" fabulous!

THANK YOU

Thank you so much for reading my book! I hope I was able to help you find your fabulous! As a special gift, I would like to offer a free discovery session (a $250 value) if you are ready to implement what you've learned in my book. I have no doubt that you are ready to explore what's been holding you back from relationship success!

To book a discovery session, please visit my website listed below.

Peace and Love!

Coach Linda

www.fabover50coaching.com

Morgan James
Speakers Group

⬏ www.TheMorganJamesSpeakersGroup.com

We connect Morgan James published
authors with live and online events
and audiences who will benefit
from their expertise.

Morgan James makes all of our titles available
through the Library for All Charity Organization.

www.LibraryForAll.org